Close Reading
with Paired Texts

Level 3

Engaging Lessons to Improve Comprehension

Authors
Lori Oczkus, M.A.
Timothy Rasinski, Ph.D.

SHELL EDUCATION

Digital Texts

To obtain digital copies of all the texts in this resource, scan the QR code or visit our website at **http://www.shelleducation.com/pared-texts/**.

Publishing Credits

Corinne Burton, M.A.Ed., *President*; Jodene Lynn Smith, M.A., *Contributing Author*; Emily R. Smith, M.A.Ed., *Content Director*; Jennifer Wilson, *Editor*; Courtney Patterson, *Multimedia Designer*; Monique Dominguez, *Production Artist*; Stephanie Bernard, *Assistant Editor*; Amber Goff, *Editorial Assistant*

Image Credits

pp. 7, 12, 16, 40, 49, 57, 66, 76, 84: iStock; pp. 21, 105: Library of Congress; p. 24: Wiki; all other images: Shutterstock

Standards

© 2004 Mid-continent Research for Education and Learning (McREL)

© 2007 Teachers of English to Speakers of Other Languages, Inc. (TESOL)

© 2007 Board of Regents of the University of Wisconsin System. World-Class Instructional Design and Assessment (WIDA)

© Copyright 2010. National Governors Association Center for Best Practices and Council of Chief State School Officers. All rights reserved. (CCSS)

Shell Education
5301 Oceanus Drive
Huntington Beach, CA 92649-1030
http://www.shelleducation.com
ISBN 978-1-4258-1359-8
© 2015 Shell Educational Publishing, Inc.

Table of Contents

About Close Reading

What Is Close Reading?

Students today need to carry a "tool kit" of effective reading strategies to help them comprehend a wide variety of texts. Close reading is one way for students to enhance their understanding especially as they read more challenging texts. The Common Core State Standards (2010) call for students to "read closely to determine what the text says explicitly and to make logical inferences from it and cite specific textual evidence when writing or speaking to support conclusions drawn from the text." Instead of skipping or glossing over difficult texts, students need to develop strategies for digging into the text on their own (Fisher and Frey 2012). Good readers dig deeper as they read and reread a text for a variety of important purposes. Close reading involves rereading to highlight, underline, reconsider points, ask and answer questions, consider author's purpose and word choice, develop appropriate oral expression and fluency, and discuss the text with others. In close reading lessons, students learn to exercise the discipline and concentration for analyzing the text at hand rather than heading off topic. Students of all ages can be taught to carefully reread challenging texts on their own for a variety of purposes.

> Close reading involves rereading to highlight, underline, reconsider points, ask and answer questions, consider author's purpose and word choice, develop appropriate oral expression and fluency, and discuss the text with others.

Reciprocal Teaching, or the "Fab Four," and Close Reading

Reciprocal teaching is a scaffolded discussion technique that involves four of the most critical comprehension strategies that good readers employ to comprehend text—**predict**, **clarify**, **question**, and **summarize** (Oczkus 2010; Palincsar and Brown 1986). We refer to the reciprocal teaching strategies as "The Fab Four" (Oczkus 2012). These strategies may be discussed in any order but must all be included in every lesson. Together the four strategies form a powerful package that strengthens comprehension. Research has found that students who engage in reciprocal teaching show improvement in as little as 15 days (Palincsar and Brown 1986) by participating more eagerly in discussions. After just three to six months they may grow one to two years in their reading levels (Rosenshine and Meister 1994; Hattie 2008).

The reciprocal teaching strategies make it a practical lesson pattern for close readings. First, students briefly glance over a text to anticipate and predict the author's purpose, topic or theme, and text organization. As students read, they make note of words or phrases they want to clarify. During questioning, students reread to ask and answer questions and provide evidence from the text. Finally, students reread again to summarize and respond to the text. Quick partner and team cooperative discussions throughout the process increase students' comprehension and critical thinking. A strong teacher think-aloud component also pushes student thinking and provides students the modeling and support they need to learn to read challenging texts on their own. The four strategies become the tool kit students rely on as they read any text closely.

What Is Reading Fluency?

Fluency refers to the ability to read and understand the words encountered in texts accurately and automatically or effortlessly (Rasinski 2010). All readers come to a text with a limited or finite amount of cognitive resources. If they have to use too much of their cognitive resources to decode the words in the text, they have less of these resources available for the more important task in reading—comprehension. Readers who are not automatic in word recognition are easy to spot. They read text slowly and laboriously, often stopping at difficult words to figure them out. Although they may be able to accurately read the words, their comprehension suffers because too much of their attention had to be devoted to word recognition and away from comprehension. So although accuracy in word recognition is good, it is not enough. Fluency also includes automaticity. Good readers are fluent readers.

Fluency also has another component. It is prosody, or expressive reading. Fluent readers read orally with expression and phrasing that reflect and enhance the meaning of the passage (Rasinski 2010). Research has demonstrated that readers who are accurate, automatic, and expressive in their oral reading tend to be readers who read orally *and* silently with good comprehension. Moreover, students who perform poorly on tests of silent reading comprehension exhibit difficulties in one or more areas of reading fluency.

By combining close teaching using reciprocal teaching strategies with fluency, we end up with greater reading benefits for students than if close reading and fluency were taught and practiced separately. It is simply more efficient, more effective, and more authentic to deal with both of these critical competencies together. We call it *synergy*. Your students will call it *fun*!

Fluency and Close Reading

How does a person become fluent? The simple answer is practice. However, there are various forms of practice in reading that nurture fluency in students. Students need to hear and talk about fluent reading from and with more proficient readers. In doing so, they develop an understanding of what actually constitutes fluent reading.

Fluency should be an essential part of close reading. Without some degree of fluency, it is difficult for students to successfully engage in close reading. If readers have to invest too much cognitive energy into the lower-level tasks of word recognition, they will have less energy available for the tasks required of close reading—interpreting author's purpose, noting detailed information, making inferences, etc. Close reading, by definition, requires readers to read a text more than once for different purposes. Reading a text more than once is called *repeated reading*. Moreover, one of the purposes for repeated reading can and should be to read a passage with a level of fluency that reflects the meaning of the text (Rasinski and Griffith 2010). For fluency strategies to use with students, see page 124.

About Close Reading (cont.)

Why Pair Fiction and Nonfiction Texts?

Standards point out that from the initial stages of literacy development, students need exposure to both fiction and nonfiction texts. Yet the previous conventional wisdom was to focus primarily on fiction and gradually move toward more nonfiction. We provide a balance of the two texts throughout this book. In doing so, we give students opportunities to explore and gain proficiency in close reading strategies with a range of text types.

When pairing texts, we also provide a content connection between them. One passage can help build background knowledge while the other passage focuses on building interest. Our paired texts allow students to engage in comparing and contrasting various types of texts, which in itself is a form of close reading.

The pairing of texts also helps students see that different forms of texts may require different levels or types of reading fluency. Fiction, including poetry, is written with voice. Authors and poets try to embed a voice in their writing that they wish the reader to hear. Texts written with voice should be read with expression. Thus, these texts lend themselves extremely well to reading with appropriate fluency. While nonfiction may also be written with voice, it is a different type of writing that often requires a different form of expression and fluency. By pairing these forms of texts, we offer students opportunities to master fluent reading in two forms.

Since multiple reading encounters with the same text are required in close reading activities, you will notice the texts are not very long. Students will be able to reread the engaging texts for multiple purposes to achieve greater success with their comprehension of the texts.

Close Reading and Differentiation

The close reading lessons in this resource are filled with many options for scaffolding to meet the needs of all students, including English language learners and struggling readers. The lessons offer a variety of stopping points where the teacher can choose to think aloud and provide specific modeling, coaching, and feedback. Understanding your students' background knowledge and interests will help you decide whether you should read the informational texts first or grab students' interest by starting with the fictional texts. Throughout the lessons, vocabulary is addressed in a variety of creative ways that will help students who struggle to better understand the text. Sentence frames, such as *I think I will learn _____ because_____* or *I didn't get the word _____, so I _____,* provide students with a focus for their rereading tasks and discussions with peers. Creative options for rereading the texts to build fluency and comprehension give students who need more support lots of meaningful practice.

About Close Reading (cont.)

Effective Tips for Close Reading Lessons

To make the most out of close reading lessons, be sure to include the following:

1. **Text Focus**

   Throughout the lessons, keep the main focus on the text itself by examining how it is organized, the author's purpose, text evidence, and reasons why the author chose certain words or visuals.

2. **Think Alouds**

   Model close reading using teacher think alouds to help make thinking visible to students. For example, before asking students to find words to clarify, demonstrate by choosing a word from the text and showing different ways to clarify it.

3. **Cooperative Learning**

   Students' comprehension increases when they discuss the reading with others. Ask partners or groups to "turn and talk" during every step of the lesson.

4. **Scaffolding**

   Some students need extra support with comprehension or fluency. Use the suggestions on pages 123–124 that include sentence frames, ways to reread the text, props, gestures, and other ideas to reach every learner and make the lessons engaging.

5. **Metacognition/Independence**

   Name the rereading steps for students throughout the lessons. This will help them remember how to read closely when they encounter rigorous texts on their own. For example, before questioning say, "Now let's reread the text to find evidence as we ask and answer our questions."

Adapted from Lori D. Oczkus (2010)

A Close Reading Snapshot

Below is an example showing what one lesson might look like.

Students gather on the rug with clipboards, crayons, and copies of the poem "Planting, Waiting, Growing" by Miriam Myers. Mr. Jimenez projects a copy of the poem as students study the title and pair share predictions. Students read the poem and underline one word each that they already know and circle words that they want to learn. The class reads the poem multiple times, paying attention to the stanza breaks. In subsequent rereadings, pairs discuss the question frame *Why did the author use the word _____ to describe _____?* Partners sketch drawings to summarize the events in the poem.

Lesson Plan Overview

Teacher Pages

The lessons have overview pages that include summaries of the themes students will focus on and and answer keys. Each lesson include two Teacher Notes charts, one for the nonfiction text and one for the fiction text. Both charts follow the same structure as below. **Note:** You will find some teacher modeling suggestions in the right hand columns of the charts. Prior to implementing the lessons, provide students with copies of the texts to mark throughout the lessons, and project larger versions of the texts for the class to see so that you can model important steps in the close-reading process. You can find digital copies of the texts at **http://www.shelleducation.com/paired-texts/**.

Lesson Steps	Purpose

Ready, Set, Predict!	In this section, students will:
	• skim the text
	• anticipate the topic
	    • think about the author's purpose
	    • think about text organization

Go!	In this section, students will:
	• read the text independently
	• anticipate the topic
	• think about the author's purpose
	    • think about text organization
	    • listen to the teacher read the text aloud
	    • reread the text for various purposes
	    • focus on various aspects of fluency

Reread to Clarify	In this section, students will: • work independently, in pairs, or in small groups to reread the text and identify words or phrases they want to clarify • use various clarifying strategies such as sounding out, studying word parts, visualizing content, and rereading
Reread to Question	In this section, students will: • work independently, in pairs, or in small groups to reread the text and ask and answer questions about the text • use text evidence to answer questions that are self-generated or asked by the teacher
Reread to Summarize and Respond	In this section, students will: • work independently, in pairs, or in small groups to reread the text and summarize the main ideas and details • evaluate the text • share text evidence to support their summaries of the text

Lesson Plan Overview (cont.)

Student Pages

After reading each pair of fiction and nonfiction texts, the lesson plan continues with opportunities for comparing the two texts and creative follow-up options that can be conducted with the whole class, small groups, partners, or as independent work in a center.

Response Pages

Each text has a follow-up activity page where students use their knowledge of the text to answer text-dependent questions.

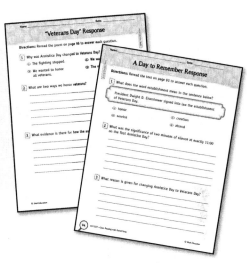

Comparing the Texts

This activity page offers creative reasons for students to reread both texts and synthesize information from both to accomplish a task. A few examples include: writing a news account, writing a poem, filling in a graphic organizer, or making a game.

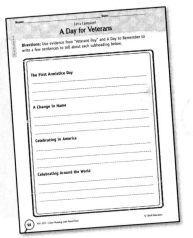

All About the Content

This activity page offers four activities that students can choose from that focus on their comprehension of the paired texts. The activities have the same focus in each lesson: reading, fluency, word study, and writing.

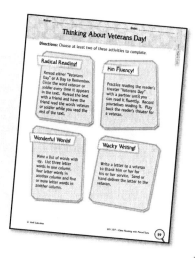

Benjamin Franklin

Theme Summary

Benjamin Franklin—few people have had such an important influence in so many areas of our lives. He was an inventor, a discoverer, and even a founding father. Students will read an informational text and a poem about Franklin, which will help them learn about the great things Franklin accomplished. Who knows, this text pair may inspire the next influential inventor in your classroom!

Answer Key

"The Great Benjamin Franklin" Response (page 13)

1. B. He invented the lightning rod.

2. Franklin helped write the Declaration of Independence and the Constitution, which helped establish the United States of America as its own country.

3. Benjamin Franklin had significant contributions as a scientist, an inventor, and a founding father.

"Curious Ben" Response (page 16)

1. B. curious

2. Answers may vary. Students should use the text to explain that many of the discoveries and inventions Benjamin Franklin made were in the area of science.

3. The author likes Benjamin Franklin. The text says that Benjamin Franklin was an inspiration. The author also tells about all the good things he invented and discovered.

Let's Compare! Inventor, Discoverer, Author (page 17)

Students' paragraphs will vary but should include some of the following for each section: **Invented**—lightning rod, batteries, fire department, lending library, open stove, bifocal glasses, and the political cartoon; **Discovered**—lightning is electricity; **Wrote**—helped write the Declaration of Independence and the United States Constitution.

Standards

➡ Refer to parts of stories, dramas, and poems when writing or speaking about a text, using terms such as chapter, scene, and stanza; describe how each successive part builds on earlier sections.

➡ Use text features and search tools (e.g., key words, sidebars, hyperlinks) to locate information relevant to a given topic efficiently.

➡ Read on-level text with purpose and understanding.

Materials

➡ The Great Benjamin Franklin (pages 12–13)

➡ "The Great Benjamin Franklin" Response (page 13)

➡ Curious Ben (page 15)

➡ "Curious Ben" Response (page 16)

➡ Let's Compare! Inventor, Discoverer, Author (page 17)

➡ Thinking About Benjamin Franklin! (page 18)

➡ pencils

➡ index cards

➡ drawing paper

➡ colored pencils

Comparing the Texts

After students complete the lessons for each text, have them work in pairs or groups to reread both texts and complete the Let's Compare! Inventor, Discoverer, Author activity page (page 17). Finally, students can work to complete the Thinking About Benjamin Franklin! matrix (page 18). The activities allow students to work on the important literacy skills of reading, writing, vocabulary, and fluency.

Nonfiction Text Teacher Notes
The Great Benjamin Franklin

	Lesson Steps	Teacher Think Alouds
Ready, Set, Predict!	• Provide students with the text and display a larger version. Ask students to share what they notice about how the text is organized. • Ask students to anticipate the author's purpose in writing the text and to predict what it is about.	"I notice this text has subheadings. These headings will help me know what to expect when reading this text."
Go!	• Have students do a quick and quiet text walk with pencils in hand. Ask them to put exclamation marks next to words they find interesting or challenging. • Read the text aloud to students. Model fluent reading to convey meaning and keep interest. • Place students in groups of five. Have groups practice reading the text together.	"Notice how I read the first two sentences in the section *Scientist and Inventor*. I try to make my voice sound happy because Benjamin Franklin's inventions made life better for the people at the time and also for us today!"
Reread to Clarify	• Have students reread the text and circle any words or ideas they want to clarify. Provide time for students to discuss strategies for clarifying the words they circled with small groups. • Ask students to circle the subheadings. Have them read the paragraphs under the subheadings and underline the sentences that best clarify the subheadings.	"I don't get the word *Massachusetts*, so I ask a friend. She pronounces the word for me slowly and clearly. Now, I recognize it as a name of a state."
Reread to Question	• Explain to students that they will reread the text to ask and answer questions about it. • Provide each student with an index card. Have them write questions that can be answered within each section of the text. Collect the questions. Assign each section a number (1, 2, or 3). Ask a question. Have students show you the number of fingers to indicate which section the answer is found in. Select students to provide the text evidence that answers the question. • Have students respond to the question and prompts on page 13.	
Reread to Summarize and Respond	• Provide drawing paper to students. Tell students to reread the text with partners to summarize by creating timelines of Franklin's life. • Review the close reading strategies with students by singing the song on page 128.	

*Note: For more tips, engagement strategies, and fluency options to include in this lesson, see pages 122–128.

The Great Benjamin Franklin

Adapted from a piece by Lisa Zamosky

Benjamin Franklin is one of the greatest Americans in history. Growing up, his family didn't have much money, but through hard work, he became very successful at many things.

Early Life

Benjamin Franklin was born January 17, 1706, in Boston, Massachusetts. He stopped going to school at age 10 to work with his father. At 13, he went to work for his older brother, James, who owned a printing house. When Franklin grew older, he also owned his own publishing house.

Scientist and Inventor

Benjamin Franklin was also a scientist. He invented many new things that made people's lives better. When Franklin was 42 years old, he sold his printing business. He wanted to follow his love of science. In 1747, he learned that lightning was electricity. He learned this by flying a kite with a key tied to the string under a thundercloud. When he touched the key, he got a shock. This shock proved lightning is electricity. After this test, he created the lightning rod. This is a metal bar that is put on houses or other buildings. Lightning hits the rod instead of the buildings. Franklin saved many lives with this invention. He invented many other things important to us today, as well. He invented the open stove, bifocal glasses, and the political cartoon.

Founding Father

When Benjamin Franklin was born, Massachusetts was one of just 13 colonies. The colonies were ruled by Great Britain. He was one of the people who helped the United States of America become a country. He helped to write the Declaration of Independence. This said that the American colonies were no longer part of Great Britain. He also helped write the United States Constitution. Benjamin Franklin is known as one of America's Founding Fathers.

Curious Ben

by Linda Arnold

Who invented the lightning rod?
Ben Franklin, that's who!
Who invented batteries?
Ben Franklin did that, too!

Curious Ben, Curious Ben,
Science was the key
That helped you on your way
With each discovery.

Who invented the fire department?
Ben Franklin, that's who!
And the lending library?
Ben Franklin did that, too!

Curious Ben, Curious Ben
You're an inspiration
Always full of bright ideas
That helped to build our nation.

Who invented the lightning rod?
Ben Franklin, that's who!
If we find a bright idea
We can be inventors, too!

Language Arts Texts

Language Arts Texts

"Curious Ben" Response

Directions: Reread the poem on page 15 to answer each question.

1. What word does the author use to describe Franklin's personality?

   Ⓐ inventor

   Ⓑ curious

   Ⓒ discoverer

   Ⓓ scientist

2. The author uses the phrase *Science was the key.* Use the text to explain what this means.

   _____

   _____

   _____

   _____

   _____

3. What does the author think of Benjamin Franklin? Use the text to tell how you know.

   _____

   _____

   _____

Let's Compare!

Inventor, Discoverer, Author

Directions: Reread "Curious Ben" and "The Great Benjamin Franklin." Write a short paragraph in each box telling what Benjamin Franklin invented, discovered, and wrote.

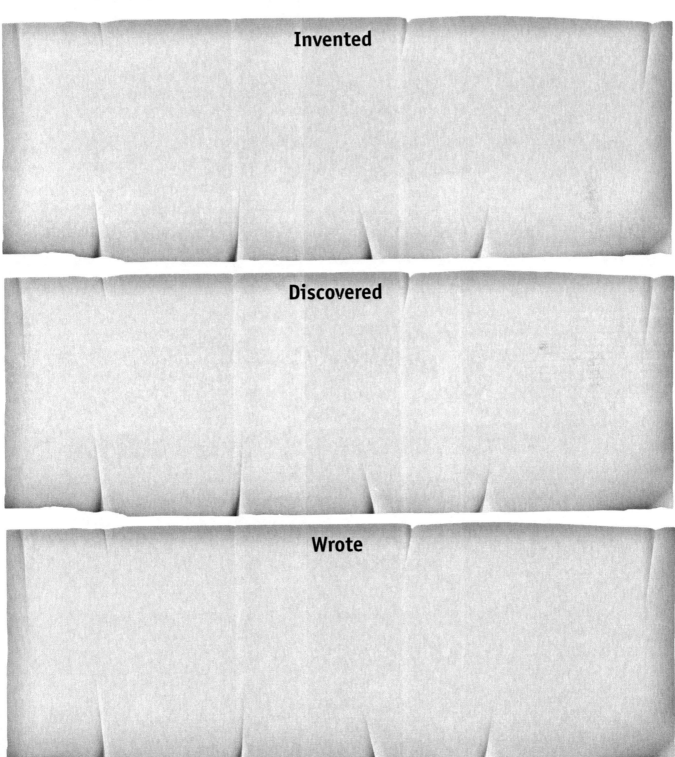

Invented

Discovered

Wrote

Thinking About Benjamin Franklin!

Directions: Choose at least two of these activities to complete.

Radical Reading

Practice reading "Curious Ben" with a partner. One person can read the parts of the poem that repeat in each stanza. The other person can read the rest of the poem. Practice until you can read the poem fluently together. Then, switch roles.

Fun Fluency

Practice reading "The Great Benjamin Franklin." Once you are fluent at reading it, record yourself. Play it back for a partner.

Wonderful Words

Write the word *invention* at the top of a sheet of paper. Make as many words as you can from the letters in the word *invention*. Give yourself 2 points for every 2-letter word, 3 points for every 3-letter word, and so on. Total your points. Try to score at least 20 points.

Wacky Writing

Choose one of the things Benjamin Franklin invented, and draw a picture of it. Then, write about how and why it is still important today.

Unit 2 Overview
Helen Keller

Theme Summary

She became blind and deaf at age one, yet Helen Keller became a hero to the world. Students will read about the life of Helen Keller in a nonfiction text and about her inspirational teacher, Anne Sullivan, in a poem.

Standards

➡ Describe characters in a story (e.g., their traits, motivations, or feelings) and explain how their actions contribute to the sequence of events.

➡ Ask and answer questions to demonstrate understanding of a text, referring explicitly to the text as the basis for the answers.

➡ Use context to confirm or self-correct word recognition and understanding, rereading as necessary.

Materials

➡ *The Life of Helen Keller* (page 21)

➡ *"The Life of Helen Keller" Response* (page 22)

➡ *A Very Special Teacher* (page 24)

➡ *"A Very Special Teacher" Response* (page 25)

➡ *Let's Compare! Anne Sullivan* (page 26)

➡ *Thinking About Helen Keller!* (page 27)

➡ pencils

➡ writing paper

Comparing the Texts

After students complete the lessons for each text, have them work in pairs or groups to reread both texts and complete the *Let's Compare! Anne Sullivan* activity page (page 26). Finally, students can work to complete the *Thinking About Helen Keller!* matrix (page 27). The activities allow students to work on the important literacy skills of reading, writing, vocabulary, and fluency.

Answer Key

"The Life of Helen Keller" Response (page 22)

1. B. She was frustrated because she could not hear or see.

2. Anne Sullivan had Helen Keller feel her lips as she spoke. She taught Keller new words and how to connect ideas.

3. Keller did not let being blind and deaf hold her back from going to college, writing books, or traveling. She taught others to respect blind and deaf people.

"A Very Special Teacher" Response (page 25)

1. C. a guide

2. Answers will vary. Students may mention the following phrases in their responses: *Someone who stands beside you, helps you round each bend,* and *caring.*

3. Answers will vary. Students may say that a special teacher guides us and helps us on our way.

Let's Compare! Anne Sullivan (page 26)

Student responses will vary but may include some of the following: "The Life of Helen Keller" helps us to understand who "A Very Special Teacher" is about because it talks about Keller's family needing help and hiring a teacher. The poem refers to *a special teacher* throughout. The line *A strong but caring teacher can be just like a guide* in the poem can be understood in the nonfiction text because it states that Keller would feel Sullivan's lips and copy her.

Nonfiction Text Teacher Notes
The Life of Helen Keller

	Lesson Steps	Teacher Think Alouds
Ready, Set, Predict!	• Read the title aloud to students. Have them predict the author's purpose in writing the text based on the title using the following: *I think the author wrote this text to _____* (e.g., *inform, entertain, persuade*) *because _____*. • Provide students with the text and display a larger version.	"I think the author wrote this text to inform because the title says it is about the life of a person who existed."
Go!	• Have students read the text independently. • Then, read the text aloud to students as they follow along, modeling expressive reading. • Discuss with students the author's purpose and what evidence there is to support students' ideas of the author's purpose. • Reread the text chorally.	
Reread to Clarify	• Have students reread the text with partners to circle words they want to clarify. Ask partners to discuss strategies for figuring out the words they identify. • Ask students to reread the text and identify two places in it that help them to visualize. Provide time for students to discuss their ideas with partners.	"I have trouble reading the word *tantrums*, so I look for parts of the word I know. I see the word *tan*. Then, I sound out the end of the word *-trums*. *Drums* is almost the same as *-trums*. Now, the word makes sense to me."
Reread to Question	• Explain to students that they will reread the text to ask and answer questions. • Divide the class into five groups. Assign each group a question word: *who, what, where, why,* and *when*. Ask them to write one or two questions using their assigned words. Invite them to read their questions aloud so the rest of the class can answer them. • Have students respond to the question and prompts on page 22.	
Reread to Summarize and Respond	• Tell students to reread the text to summarize. • Provide students with paper that has been folded in half. On one half, students should write about what Keller's life was like before she met Anne Sullivan. On the other half, students should write about what Keller's life was like after she met Anne Sullivan.	"As I reread to summarize the text, I will highlight the information that tells about Keller before she met Sullivan, such as she could not talk to people, and I will underline the information that tells about Keller after she met Sullivan, such as she learned new words."

*Note: For more tips, engagement strategies, and fluency options to include in this lesson, see pages 122–128.

The Life of Helen Keller

Helen Keller was born in 1880. She was a healthy baby. The first year of her life was normal. One day, she got really sick. She had a very high fever. She lost her sight. She also lost her hearing. She was blind and deaf.

Keller grew very frustrated. She could not hear. She could not see. She could not talk to people. Keller began to have horrible tantrums.

Keller's family needed help. They hired a teacher. Anne Sullivan became Keller's teacher. She taught Keller many things, including new words. She also helped Keller connect ideas. Keller felt Sullivan's lips as she talked. Even though Sullivan was not always easy to understand, Keller never gave up.

Keller worked hard her entire life. She grew up to be an amazing woman. She went to college. She wrote books. She traveled the world. She did not let anything stop her.

Perhaps Keller's greatest gift was teaching others to respect her. She wanted respect for all people who were blind or deaf. She shared her life with others. Helen Keller died in 1968. She lived a full life. She was a hero to many people.

"The Life of Helen Keller" Response

Directions: Reread the text on page 21 to answer each question.

1. What evidence is there for why Keller had horrible tantrums?

   Ⓐ She got really sick and had a high fever.

   Ⓒ She worked hard her entire life.

   Ⓑ She was frustrated because she could not hear or see.

   Ⓓ Her family needed help.

2. Describe how Anne Sullivan helped Helen Keller.

   _____

   _____

   _____

   _____

   _____

3. The last line of the text states that Helen Keller *was a hero to many people.* What evidence is there for why she would be a hero?

   _____

   _____

   _____

   _____

   _____

Fiction Text Teacher Notes

A Very Special Teacher

	Lesson Steps	Teacher Think Alouds
Ready, Set, Predict!	• Provide students with the text and display a larger version. Ask them to preview it to determine what type of text it is. Ask students to turn to partners and discuss the following: *I think the author wrote this to _____ (e.g., inform, entertain, persuade) because _____.*	"When I see short lines, I immediately think that the text may be a poem. I can tell by reading the first few lines of the text that this text rhymes."
Go!	• Tell students to read the poem independently with a pencil in hand. Ask students to circle any words they do not know or words they want to know. • Read the poem aloud to students. • Ask students to review the predictions they made about the author's purpose. Have them discuss whether or not they need to revise their ideas based on new evidence from the text. Ask them to box evidence in the poem to support their responses.	
Reread to Clarify	• Have students discuss the words and ideas they want to clarify with partners. Encourage them to use more than one reading strategy to determine the meaning of unknown words (e.g., *sounding out, rereading, using syllables*). • Invite students to reread the poem and underline any words or phrases that are used to describe a teacher.	"I don't understand the part of the poem where it says, *you're standing in the darkness*, so I read on and see the line *Into that brighter day*. By reading the text between the two lines, I see that a teacher can help a person's day become brighter."
Reread to Question	• Pair students to reread the poem to question. Tell them to ask two questions each about it. Provide stems to help them: *What does the author mean by _____?* and *Find evidence to support your thoughts about _____.* • Have students respond to the question and prompts on page 25.	
Reread to Summarize and Respond	• Provide students with writing paper folded in half. Have them reread the poem to summarize by writing words from the poem that describe special teachers on one side. Then, ask them to describe very special teachers in their own words on the other side.	"When I read a poem about a topic, such as a teacher, I try to make connections to my own life. I have experiences with teachers, so I think about what parts of the poem apply to me."

***Note:** For more tips, engagement strategies, and fluency options to include in this lesson, see pages 122–128.

Language Arts Texts

A Very Special Teacher

by Linda Arnold

A very special teacher can be just like a friend,
Someone who stands beside you
And helps you round each bend.

A strong but caring teacher can be just like a guide,
Someone who helps you see the light
That's shining deep inside.

If you're standing in the darkness
And a song of hope you cannot hear,
A true friend and teacher
Can help miracles appear.

A very special teacher can help us on our way.
But we're the ones who travel
Into that brighter day.
For every dream is possible with courage on our side,
The power of knowledge, and a teacher as our guide.

Helen Keller with Anne Sullivan.

"A Very Special Teacher" Response

Directions: Reread the poem on page 24 to answer each question.

1. What word is used to describe a teacher?

   Ⓐ a traveler   Ⓒ a guide

   Ⓑ a student   Ⓓ a dream

2. What phrase in the poem helps you to understand the simile *A very special teacher can be just like a friend*?

   _____

   _____

   _____

   _____

   _____

3. Use the text to describe what a special teacher does.

   _____

   _____

   _____

   _____

Language Arts Texts

Anne Sullivan

Directions: The poem "A Very Special Teacher" does not specifically name Anne Sullivan, but it was written about her. Describe how evidence from "The Life of Helen Keller" helps you better understand the poem.

_____

_____

_____

_____

_____

_____

_____

_____

_____

_____

_____

_____

_____

_____

_____

_____

Thinking About Helen Keller!

Directions: Choose at least two of these activities to complete.

Radical Reading

Reread "The Life of Helen Keller." Underline all the positive things Helen Keller did with her life. Compare Helen Keller to someone you know and admire. For example, you may know someone who did not give up after facing a challenging situation.

Fun Fluency

Reread the poem "A Very Special Teacher" with a friend. Take turns reading the lines. When you are fluent at reading it together, read it aloud for the class.

Wonderful Words

Make a list of words that describe a good teacher. Use words from "A Very Special Teacher" and add your own, too! Share your list with a teacher at your school.

Wacky Writing

Write a very special thank-you note to a teacher or a coach in your life who has impacted you in some positive way. Be sure to include specific examples for why you are thanking him or her.

Unit 3 Overview
School Lunches

Theme Summary

They are notorious for tasting bad, but school lunches are on the move. The movement to make school lunches healthier and tastier is growing. Students will read a poem about school lunches and read a memo about a change being made to lunches at one school. Your students will be ready to go to lunch after reading this text pair!

Answer Key

"Change Comes to School Lunches" Response (page 31)

1. C. Model eating the healthy, new lunches.

2. The lunch program is changing because obesity is a big problem, and the school lunch program has been partly to blame.

3. The principal thinks many students will like the changes right away, but it will take time for other students to get used to the changes.

"School Lunch" Response (page 34)

1. B. The person in the poem is hungry and is still in line for lunch.

2. The title has the word *school* in it. There is also a bell and a lunch line mentioned in the poem.

3. The person thinking about all the food is hungry and is still in line. So, the author uses the word *growl* to let the reader know he or she is still hungry.

Let's Compare! Make Healthy Choices (page 35)

The bolded words below represent the words that students should circle.

School Lunch	Change Comes to School Lunches
cheese	salad bar
meat	fruits
hash	vegetables
jicama	grilled chicken sandwiches
stew	fish tacos
cookie	whole wheat pasta
	tofu burgers
	potato chips
	ice cream
	baked crisps
	frozen yogurt

Standards

➠ Ask and answer questions to demonstrate understanding of a text, referring explicitly to the text as the basis for the answers.

➠ Determine the main idea of a text; recount the key details and explain how they support the main idea.

➠ Read on-level prose and poetry orally with accuracy, appropriate rate, and expression on successive readings.

Materials

➠ *Change Comes to School Lunches* (page 30)
➠ *"Change Comes to School Lunches" Response* (page 31)
➠ *School Lunch* (page 33)
➠ *"School Lunch" Response* (page 34)
➠ *Let's Compare! Make Healthy Choices* (page 35)
➠ *Thinking About School Lunches!* (page 36)
➠ pencils
➠ writing paper
➠ index cards

Comparing the Texts

After students complete the lessons for each text, have them work in pairs or groups to reread both texts and complete the *Let's Compare! Make Healthy Choices* activity page (page 35). Finally, students can work to complete the *Thinking About School Lunches!* matrix (page 36). The activities allow students to work on the important literacy skills of reading, writing, vocabulary, and fluency.

Nonfiction Text Teacher Notes
Change Comes to School Lunches

		Lesson Steps	Teacher Think Alouds
	Ready, Set, Predict!	• Provide students with the text and display a larger version. Ask them what they notice about the organization and format of the text. • Ask partners to make predictions using the following: *I think I will enjoy reading this text because _____.*	"When I look at the top of the text, I see *To: All Willowbrook Elementary Teachers and Staff*. When I look at the bottom, I see *From: Principal Warren*. This makes me think that the principal is informing the staff about something."
	Go!	• Have students read the text independently. Ask them to circle words that show the memo was written for a school. • Read the text aloud to students. Model fluent reading strategies such as phrasing. • Ask partners to identify the main idea of the memo. Then, have them reread the memo and underline sentences that include key details that support the main idea.	"Often the main idea is in the title. I am going to underline the line *On Monday, our lunch program becomes healthy* because it supports the main idea that changes are going to be made to the school lunches."
	Reread to Clarify	• Tell students to reread the text and box words they want to clarify. Ask small groups to review the strategies they use to clarify the words. • Ask students to reread the text and mark words or sentences that clarify how the lunches will change at Willowbrook School with asterisks (*).	"I don't know the word *administration*, so I look it up in the dictionary. I now know that it means 'the leaders of an organization.'"
	Reread to Question	• Pair students. Have partners reread the text to question. One student should ask *why* questions. The other student should ask *how* questions. The students should try to answer each other's questions. Invite a few pairs to share their questions out loud for the whole class to hear. Discuss the answers as a class. • Have students respond to the question and prompts on page 31.	
	Reread to Summarize and Respond	• Distribute writing paper to students. Instruct them to fold it in half. Tell students to reread the text to summarize by listing all the new, healthy foods that will be served at Willowbrook Elementary School on one side, and listing all the foods that are being replaced on the other side.	

*Note: For more tips, engagement strategies, and fluency options to include in this lesson, see pages 122–128.

Change Comes to School Lunches

To: All Willowbrook Elementary Teachers and Staff

Great news! The school administration has decided to change the school lunch program. On Monday, our lunch program becomes healthy. We'll have an organic salad bar with plenty of fresh fruits and vegetables. We'll have delicious grilled chicken sandwiches, fish tacos, and whole wheat pasta. There will be plenty of vegetarian entrées, too, like tofu burgers.

There will be no more greasy potato chips or fattening ice cream. Instead, we'll have baked crisps and frozen yogurt. The only drinks will be water, fruit juice, and skim milk. Most of the students will love these changes right away. For others, eating healthy lunches will take some time to get used to.

Obesity is a big problem on our campus, and our lunch program has been partly to blame. These changes are long overdue.

I encourage you to try all the great new foods offered for lunch. You can model healthy eating for your students!

From: Principal Warren

"Change Comes to School Lunches" Response

Directions: Reread the text on page 30 to answer each question.

1. What are the teachers supposed to do after reading this memo?

   Ⓐ Make suggestions about new lunch choices.

   Ⓒ Model eating the healthy, new lunches.

   Ⓑ Help prepare the new lunches.

   Ⓓ Help change the lunch program.

2. Why is the lunch program changing?

   _____

   _____

   _____

   _____

   _____

3. How does the principal think the students will respond to the new lunch program?

   _____

   _____

   _____

   _____

   _____

   _____

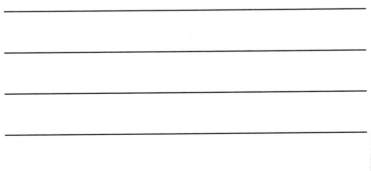

Fiction Text Teacher Notes
School Lunch

	Lesson Steps	Teacher Think Alouds

Ready, Set, Predict!

- Provide the poem to students and display a larger version. Allow time for them to skim it to determine if there is a rhyming structure.
- Ask students to work with partners to predict the author's purpose using the following: *I think the author wrote this poem to _____* (e.g., *persuade, inform, entertain*).

Go!

- Tell students to read the text independently. Ask them to use pencils to circle any words they find interesting or tricky.
- Read the poem aloud to students as they follow along. Model and discuss fluent reading strategies such as pacing.
- Have students review their predictions of the author's purpose with partners. Allow them to confirm or revise their ideas as necessary.

"I notice this poem rhymes. Knowing this helps me read the poem because I can get into a rhythm as I read it."

Reread to Clarify

- Provide time for students to reread the text and discuss the words they circled earlier. Have them work with partners as they use strategies to clarify the interesting or tricky words.
- Have students underline each food item listed in the poem and box the verb that shows how the food will be eaten. (e.g., The word *gnaw* should be boxed to represent the underlined word *jicama*.)

"The word *jicama* is tricky, so I look it up in the dictionary. I find out that it is a vegetable and that the *j* is pronounced with a /h/ not a /j/ sound."

Reread to Question

- Put students into groups of three. Distribute an index card to each group. Ask them to reread the text to question by writing three questions on the cards using the words *how, where,* and *what*. Have groups join together. Each group should ask the questions they wrote and try to answer the other groups' questions.
- Have students respond to the question and prompts on page 34.

"My first question is 'How is the yummy lunch eaten?' My second question is 'Where will I wait?' My last question is 'What will I chew?' These questions will help me remember the text."

Reread to Summarize and Respond

- Tell partners to reread the poem to summarize by pantomiming the various verbs used in it. The partners can take turns pantomiming and guessing the verbs and the foods being eaten that way.
- Review the close reading strategies with students by singing the song on page 128.

School Lunch

Hungry! I yell, "I hear the bell!"
It's time to dine. I'll wait in line!
Then . . .
I'll munch a bunch of yummy lunch.
I'll eat a treat of cheese and meat.
I'll gnash a rash of tasty hash.
I'll gnaw a paw of jicama.
I'll chew a slew of tasty stew.
I'll nip some sips of milk through lips.
I'll feed the need for cookie greed.
It's time to dine. But . . . I'm still in line!
Growl . . .

"School Lunch" Response

Directions: Reread the poem on page 33 to answer each question.

1. What is the problem in the poem?

    Ⓐ The person likes to eat many different kinds of food.

    Ⓒ The person in the poem is a bear.

    Ⓑ The person in the poem is hungry and is still in line for lunch.

    Ⓓ The person in the poem is at school.

2. What evidence is there to support that the setting of the poem is a school?

_____

_____

_____

3. Why does the author use the word *growl* at the end of the poem?

_____

_____

_____

                            _____

                            _____

                            _____

                            _____

Let's Compare!

Make Healthy Choices

Directions: Make a list of each food in "School Lunch" and "Change Comes to School Lunches." Circle the foods in each that are healthy choices.

School Lunch	Change Comes to School Lunches

Thinking About School Lunches!

Directions: Choose at least two of these activities to complete.

Radical Reading

Practice reading "School Lunch" until you can read it fluently. Then, go read it to the workers in the cafeteria at your school. You may wish to record the reading so that the cafeteria workers can listen to it at their convenience.

Fun Fluency

Practice reading "Change Comes to School Lunches" in your principal voice. Once you are fluent at reading it in that voice, go read it to the principal.

Wonderful Words

Make a list of the foods you like to eat for lunch. Circle the foods that are healthy choices. Share your list with a partner.

Wacky Writing

Write a memo to your mom or the lunch workers in your school about the lunches you eat. Let them know if you would like something to change in your lunches.

Unit 4 Overview
Multiplication

Theme Summary

Knowing multiplication facts is helpful for third graders but also for life. Students will read about multiplication in a poem and a real-life problem situation. Your students will be ready to multiply after working with this text pair!

Standards

- Ask and answer questions to demonstrate understanding of a literature text, referring explicitly to the text as the basis for the answers.
- Ask and answer questions to demonstrate understanding of an informational text, referring explicitly to the text as the basis for the answers.
- Multiply and divide whole numbers.

Materials

- *The Crayon Factory* (page 39)
- *"The Crayon Factory" Response* (page 40)
- *Math Journey* (page 42)
- *"Math Journey" Response* (page 43)
- *Let's Compare! Multiplication Rhymes* (page 44)
- *Thinking About Multiplication!* (page 45)
- pencils
- writing paper
- paper strips
- drawing paper

Comparing the Texts

After students complete the lessons for each text, have them work in pairs or groups to reread both texts and complete the *Let's Compare! Multiplication Rhymes* activity page (page 44). Finally, students can work to complete the *Thinking About Multiplication!* matrix (page 45). The activities allow students to work on the important literacy skills of reading, writing, vocabulary, and fluency.

Answer Key

"The Crayon Factory" Response (page 40)

1. A. Sam
2. Alberto wants to create a longer box.
3. Bob's design has six rows with eight crayons in each row.

"Math Journey" Response (page 43)

1. C. science
2. The text explains that math has been used *From ancient Greece to modern day*.
3. The word *key* means that it is important.

Let's Compare! Multiplication Rhymes (page 44)

Students' rhymes will vary. Check that they accurately describe the multiplication problems from "The Crayon Factory."

Nonfiction Text Teacher Notes
The Crayon Factory

		Lesson Steps	Teacher Think Alouds
	Ready, Set, Predict!	• Provide the text to students and display a larger version. Allow time for them to predict what the text will be about. • Ask partners to discuss the following: *I think the author wrote this to _____ (e.g., inform, entertain, persuade) because _____.*	
	Go!	• Allow time for students to read through the text independently. • Read the text aloud to students. Model fluent reading. Discuss how you read it fluently. • Divide students into four groups. Assign each group one of the crew members' name (e.g., *Bob, Mei, Alberto, Sam*). Have them read the lines related to the crew members they were assigned.	"There are four different ideas presented in this text. Notice how I pause in between each new idea. This helps the listener understand that an explanation of each idea is starting."
	Reread to Clarify	• Have students reread the text and underline any words or phrases they want to clarify. Ask them to work with partners to discuss strategies for clarifying the words they underline. • Write multiplication problems in the margin next to the designs suggested by the crew members.	"The word *feedback* is confusing to me, so I look it up in the dictionary and find it means 'helpful information to improve a project.'"
	Reread to Question	• Divide students into groups of four to reread to question. Have each student select one of the crew members from the text and write a question about the design that member suggested. Collect the questions, keeping the questions from each group together, and distribute them other groups. Groups should work together to answer the questions they receive. • Have students respond to the question and prompts on page 40.	
	Reread to Summarize and Respond	• Tell students to reread the text to summarize by making diagrams of the suggested boxes from the text. Then, have them write short paragraphs explaining which designs they think should be used and why. • Invite students to share their paragraphs with partners.	"When we read about so many different ways to design a crayon box, it helps me to draw a diagram, so that I can see in a picture what is being described in the text."

*Note: For more tips, engagement strategies, and fluency options to include in this lesson, see pages 122–128.

The Crayon Factory

The manager of a crayon factory has to design a new box for crayons. She has to figure out a design that will hold 48 crayons. The factory crew gives the manager some ideas.

First, Bob suggests a box with six rows. He says that there would be eight crayons in each row.

Next, Mei suggests a box with four rows. She says that there would be twelve crayons in each row.

Alberto decides he wants to create a longer box for the crayons. He wants only three rows for the box. Each row would have sixteen crayons.

Sam has one more idea. He suggests a long skinny box with only two rows. Twenty-four crayons would be in each row.

The crew is proud of their ideas, and their manager is happy to have some feedback from others. Now, she has to figure out which design would be the best to make. What do you think?

Mathematics Texts

"The Crayon Factory" Response

Directions: Reread the text on page 39 to answer each question.

1. Whose design is described as *a long skinny box*?

   Ⓐ Sam   Ⓒ Alberto

   Ⓑ Bob   Ⓓ Mei

2. How does the text describe Alberto's reason for designing a box with rows of 16 crayons?

   _____

   _____

   _____

   _____

3. Describe the design that has the fewest number of crayons in each row.

   _____

   _____

   _____

   _____

Fiction Text Teacher Notes

Math Journey

	Lesson Steps	Teacher Think Alouds
Ready, Set, Predict!	• Provide students with the text and display a larger version. Ask them to preview it to observe its rhythmical structure. • Have partners discuss the following: *I think the author wrote this to _____* (e.g., *inform, entertain, persuade*) *because _____.*	"I think the author wrote this text to entertain because it is a poem."
Go!	• Ask students to independently read the text and circle words they want to understand. • Read the poem aloud to students. Model fluent reading. Have students box the rhyming word pairs in the text.	"I notice that there are many words in this poem that rhyme. Notice how I emphasize those words when I read the poem aloud."
Reread to Clarify	• Ask students to reread the poem and underline any words they want to clarify. Provide the following prompt for them to use as they discuss strategies they use for clarifying the words they circle. *I don't get the _____* (e.g., *word, phrase, sentence, part*), *so I _____.* • Have students underline sentences in the poem that can also be written as math equations. Have students write the math equations in the margin.	
Reread to Question	• Write the words *who, what, where,* and *when* on strips of paper. Provide one strip of paper to each student. Have students reread the poem and write questions beginning with the words on their strips. Collect the questions, and redistribute them to small groups. Have the groups locate the answers in the text. • Have students respond to the question and prompts on page 43.	"To help me remember where math has come from, my question is *Where has math come from?* I read the line *From ancient Greece to modern day* and I understand that math has come from ancient Greece."
Reread to Summarize and Respond	• Provide students with drawing paper. Tell them to reread the poem to summarize by creating illustrations to go with the poem. Allow students to share their illustrations with each other along with brief explanations of their drawings.	

*Note: For more tips, engagement strategies, and fluency options to include in this lesson, see pages 122–128.

Mathematics Texts

Math Journey

by Linda Arnold

6 times 7 is 42.
Count on me, and I'll count on you,
For a journey, a math journey.
Why hesitate, just calculate.
4 times 3 times 2 times 1,
That's . . . 24!
Wasn't that fun?
Do the math, yeah! Do the math!
Math Journey!
From ancient Greece to modern day,
Math has helped science on its way.
Math is a tool. Math is a key.
Math is an opportunity!

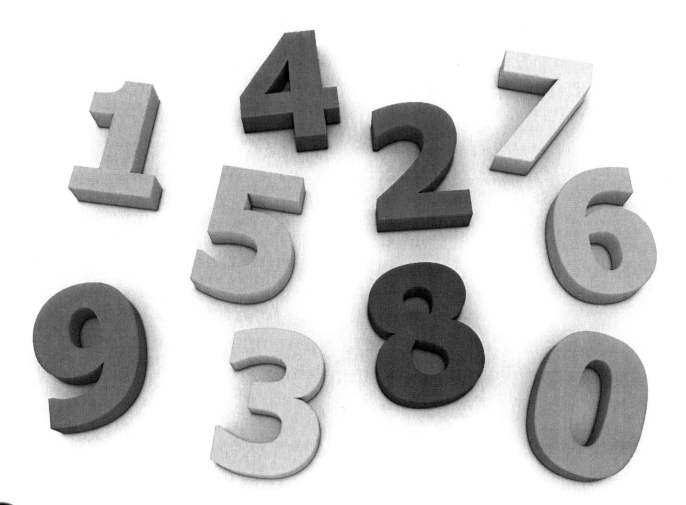

"Math Journey" Response

Directions: Reread the poem on page 42 to answer each question.

1. What has math helped?

    Ⓐ ancient Greece   Ⓒ science

    Ⓑ modern day   Ⓓ a journey

2. How does the text describe the long history of math?

_____

_____

_____

_____

_____

3. What does the word *key* mean in the context of this poem?

_____

_____

_____

_____

_____

Let's Compare!
Multiplication Rhymes

Directions: Learning rhymes can help you learn multiplication. Read the rhymes from "Math Journey." Then, write your own rhymes for the multiplication problems from "The Crayon Factory."

Math Journey
6 times 7 is 42. Count on me, and I'll count on you
4 times 3 times 2 times 1, That's...24! Wasn't that fun?

The Crayon Factory
6 times 8 equals 48
4 times 12 equals 48
3 times 16 equals 48
2 times 24 equals 48

Hint: You can rewrite the fact. For example, 6 times 8 equals 48 can also be 48 equals 8 times 6 or 48 equals 6 times 8.

Thinking About Multiplication!

Directions: Choose at least two of these activities to complete.

Radical Reading

Practice reading "Math Journey" as a rap. After you are able to read it fluently, perform it for a small group or the class.

Fun Fluency

Rewrite "The Crayon Factory" as a reader's theater script. Add dialogue to it. Practice your version with several friends reading each of the parts. Perform it for the class.

Wonderful Words

Use crayons to write the multiplication facts for three in words (for example, 3 times 3 equals 9). Use a different color for each fact.

Wacky Writing

Write a paragraph describing the various box designs that could be made for 24 crayons. Include which design you think is the best and why.

Mountain Heights

Mathematics Texts

Theme Summary

Tall mountains terrify some people and mesmerize others. Students will learn about some of the tallest mountains in the world by reading a reader's theater script and an informational text. Look out, a mountaineer may emerge from among your students after reading this text pair!

Answer Key

"Earth's Tallest Mountains" Response (page 49)

1. B. Has anyone climbed Mount Everest?

2. Although Mauna Kea is taller than Mount Everest, Mount Everest is considered the world's highest mountain because much of Mauna Kea is below the ocean.

3. Erosion can cause mountains to get smaller because *rain, snow, and ice break up the rock*. The rocks fall away or wash away, so the mountain gets smaller.

"Who's Right?" Response (page 52)

1. C. looked at a chart in a book

2. Part of Mauna Kea is above the ocean and part of it is below the ocean, which cannot be seen.

3. They are all right because one student names the tallest mountain in the United States, one student names the tallest mountain in the world that is above the ocean, and one student names the tallest mountain in the world that is both above and below the ocean.

Let's Compare! New Information (page 53)

Students' paragraphs will vary but should include information about mountains throughout the world.

Standards

➡ Ask and answer questions to demonstrate understanding of a text, referring explicitly to the text as the basis for the answers.

➡ Use text features and search tools (e.g., key words, sidebars, hyperlinks) to locate information relevant to a given topic efficiently.

➡ Understand the basic meaning of place value.

Materials

➡ *Earth's Tallest Mountains* (page 48)
➡ *"Earth's Tallest Mountains" Response* (page 49)
➡ *Who's Right?* (pages 51–52)
➡ *"Who's Right?" Response* (page 52)
➡ *Let's Compare! New Information* (page 53)
➡ *Thinking About Mountains!* (page 54)
➡ pencils
➡ writing paper
➡ index cards

Comparing the Texts

After students complete the lessons for each text, have them work in pairs or groups to reread both texts and complete the *Let's Compare! New Information* activity page (page 53). Finally, students can work to complete the *Thinking About Mountains!* matrix (page 54). The activities allow students to work on the important literacy skills of reading, writing, vocabulary, and fluency.

Earth's Tallest Mountains

	Lesson Steps	Teacher Think Alouds
Ready, Set, Predict!	• Provide the text to students and display a larger version. Ask them to skim the text and predict what it will be about. • Have partners discuss the following: *I think the author will use high-level vocabulary in this passage because _____.*	"I think the author will use high-level vocabulary in this passage because I see the definitions of two words in a box at the bottom of the page."
Go!	• Ask students to read through the text independently. Have them circle any words that are challenging as they read. • Read the text aloud to students. Model emphasizing the titles of the subheadings by pausing before and after you read them. • Divide students into four groups. Assign each group one section of text. Reread the text with each group reading its part.	
Reread to Clarify	• Ask partners to reread the text and box any words they want to clarify. Have them discuss strategies they use to figure out the tricky or confusing words. • Have students underline the sentences that have the words *summited* and *erosion* in them. Have them draw quick pictures of the words.	"I pay close attention to vocabulary words *sumitted* and *erosion*. I see that they are defined in the text. Understanding these words helps me to better understand the text."
Reread to Question	• Divide students into groups of four. Assign each student one section of the text. Provide index cards to students. Have them reread their sections and write questions about them. • Collect the cards. Ask the questions aloud. Have students predict which sections the answers are located in. Then, have students discuss the answers to the questions. • Have students respond to the question and prompts on page 49.	
Reread to Summarize and Respond	• Distribute paper to students. Tell them to fold it into four sections and write each subheading in a section. Then, ask students to reread the text to summarize by writing one sentence in each section that best describes that subheading. Ask students to turn to partners and share.	"When I see a text divided into sections, I try to understand each section and say the main point of the section in my own words."

*Note: For more tips, engagement strategies, and fluency options to include in this lesson, see pages 122–128.

Earth's Tallest Mountains

Where is the "Top of the World"?

The "Top of the World" is a nickname for Mount Everest. It is the highest mountain on Earth above sea level. It stands about 29,035 feet (8,850 meters) high. It towers over the nation of Nepal in Asia.

Has anyone climbed Mount Everest?

In 1953, two climbers summited Mount Everest. They were Edmund Hillary and Tenzing Norgay. Since then, thousands of climbers have reached the top. However, it is very dangerous, and hundreds of people have died trying to do so.

What is the tallest mountain on Earth?

The tallest mountain on Earth is Mauna Kea in Hawaii. It stands on the ocean floor, so most of it is under water. It is 33,476 feet high (10,203 meters) from its base to its top. Although it is much taller than Mount Everest, it is not the highest mountain on Earth because so little of it appears above sea level. That is why Mount Everest is considered the world's highest mountain.

Can mountains grow?

Some mountains are growing. Rocks under the earth move and push up the mountains. In fact, each year, even Mount Everest grows taller. Some mountains get smaller over time due to erosion. Rain, snow, and ice break up the rock. As these rocks fall or wash away, the mountain loses height.

> **erosion**—the process by which the earth's surface is worn away by the action of water, glaciers, and wind
>
> **summited**—reached the top of a mountain

"Earth's Tallest Mountains" Response

Directions: Reread the text on page 48 to answer each question.

1. In which section do you find the names of mountain climbers?

   Ⓐ Where is the "Top of the World"?

   Ⓒ What is the tallest mountain on Earth?

   Ⓑ Has anyone climbed Mount Everest?

   Ⓓ Can mountains grow?

2. Why is Mount Everest considered the world's highest mountain?

   _____

   _____

   _____

   _____

3. Describe how mountains can get smaller.

   _____

   _____

   _____

   _____

Fiction Text Teacher Notes
Who's Right?

	Lesson Steps	Teacher Think Alouds
Ready, Set, Predict!	• Provide the text to students and display a larger version. Have them skim over it. Discuss the format of a reader's theater script with students. • Have partners make predictions using the following: *I think the author wrote this text to _____* (e.g., *entertain, inform, persuade*) *because _____.*	
Go!	• Allow time for students to read through the text independently. Encourage them to put question marks next to words they don't know. • Read the text aloud to students. Model using different voices for each character. • Discuss the author's purpose for writing this text. Have students review or revise their predictions from earlier. • Divide students into groups of four and assign each person a character from the text. Have students practice reading the reader's theater script together with their groups.	"This is an interesting text because it is fun and entertaining to read. But I also learn information about mountain heights in it, so I think the author had two purposes for writing it."
Reread to Clarify	• Ask partners to reread the text and circle any words or sentences they want to clarify. • Have students return to the text and box the heights of the mountains in the text.	"The names of the mountains are difficult for me to read, so I break them down into small parts."
Reread to Question	• Put students into groups of four. Assign each member a character from the text. Invite other members to reread the text and ask questions about their assigned character lines. Other members must try to answer them. • Have students respond to the question and prompts on page 52.	
Reread to Summarize and Respond	• Pair students. Invite them to work together to reread the text to summarize by creating tables with the mountain names in one column and the heights listed in another column. Encourage students to put the locations of the mountains, too.	"When so much information is in a text, sometimes I have to make a list or a table so that I can look at the information in another way."

*Note: For more tips, engagement strategies, and fluency options to include in this lesson, see pages 122–128.

Who's Right?

Allison: I'm right!

Daniel: No, I'm right!

Ava: No, no, no! You're both wrong. I'm the one who's right!

Teacher: Wait a minute! What in the world are all of you right about?

Allison: We're trying to answer the question, what is the tallest mountain? I know I'm right because Mount Everest is the tallest mountain.

Daniel: Nope, Mount McKinley is the tallest mountain! It's also known by its native name, Denali, which means "the great one!"

Ava: You are both wrong because Mauna Kea is the tallest!

Teacher: I think I see the problem. I have a book that will help solve it. Look here, this book has a chart that shows the heights of the tallest mountains in the world.

Ava: It says that Mauna Kea is the tallest mountain in the world!

Teacher: You are right, but we can only see 13,803 feet (4,207 meters) of it! Most of it is below the ocean.

Allison: So Mount Everest is the tallest mountain?

Teacher: It is considered the tallest mountain. It's almost over 29,000 feet (8,840 meters) tall, but there is a way that Daniel is right, too!

Students: There is?

Teacher: You said the question was, "What is the tallest mountain?" Well, Mount McKinley is 20,329 feet (6,196 meters) tall and it is the tallest mountain in the United States.

Daniel: Yes! I knew I was right!

Who's Right? (cont)

Ava   It also says Mount Huascaran is the tallest mountain in South America at 22,205 feet (6,768 meters).

Daniel: Kilimanjaro at 19,340 feet (5,894 meters) is the tallest in Africa!

Allison: This doesn't help us answer the question. Which is the tallest?

Teacher: Actually, it does. Mauna Kea is the tallest if you measure from the ocean floor, Mount Everest is the tallest mountain on the land in all Earth, and Mount McKinley is the tallest in the United States. So, do you know what that means?

Students: We are ALL right!

• •

"Who's Right?" Response

Directions: Reread the script on pages 51–52 to answer each question.

1. How did the teacher help the children solve their problem?

   Ⓐ answered their questions   Ⓒ looked at a chart in a book

   Ⓑ stopped the argument   Ⓓ found the tallest mountain

2. Describe why we cannot see all of Mauna Kea.

   _____

   _____

3. In what way are all three students right?

   _____

   _____

   _____

Let's Compare!

New Information

Directions: Use information from "Who's Right?" to add another paragraph with the subheading shown below to "Earth's Tallest Mountains."

Mountains throughout the world

_____

_____

_____

_____

_____

_____

_____

Name: _____   Date: _____

Thinking About Mountains!

Directions: Choose at least two of these activities to complete.

Radical Reading

Reread both "Who's Right?" and "Earth's Tallest Mountains." Make illustrations showing the mountains named in the texts from shortest to tallest. Include the height of each mountain.

Fun Fluency

Practice reading "Who's Right?" with a group of friends or by yourself using different voices. After you have practiced and sound fluent, perform your version for another class or small group.

Wonderful Words

Reread both texts. Find five words that you are not sure of the definitions for. Create a definition box such as the one in "Earth's Tallest Mountains" to show the definitions.

Wacky Writing

Rewrite the information from "Earth's Tallest Mountains" in the format of a reader's theater script. Read your new version aloud to the class.

Measurement

Theme Summary

Updating the look of a room is a lot of fun, but also a lot of work! Students will find out just how much work it is by reading about a boy who wants to paint his room. Besides all the physical work, the boy must measure to find out how much paint he needs. Students will learn about how to measure perimeter by reading this text pair. Hide your tape measures—after reading this text pair, students will want to measure everything in sight!

Standards

⟹ Describe characters in a story (e.g., their traits, motivations, or feelings) and explain how their actions contribute to the sequence of events.

⟹ Use information gained from illustrations (e.g., maps, photographs) and the words in a text to demonstrate understanding of the text (e.g., where, when, why, and how key events occur).

⟹ Understand the basic measures perimeter, area, volume, capacity, mass, angle, and circumference.

Materials

⟹ *Understanding Perimeter* (page 57)

⟹ *"Understanding Perimeter" Response* (page 58)

⟹ *Painting a Room* (page 60)

⟹ *"Painting a Room" Response* (page 61)

⟹ *Let's Compare! How Big Is the Room?* (page 62)

⟹ *Thinking About Measurement!* (page 63)

⟹ pencils

⟹ tape measure

Comparing the Texts

After students complete the lessons for each text, have them work in pairs or groups to reread both texts and complete the *Let's Compare! How Big Is the Room?* activity page (page 62). Finally, students can work to complete the *Thinking About Measurement!* matrix (page 63). The activities allow students to work on the important literacy skills of reading, writing, vocabulary, and fluency.

Answer Key

"Understanding Perimeter" Response (page 58)

1. B. The distance around the sides of his garden.

2. To find the perimeter of an object, you add the lengths of each side so that you can find the distance around the edges of the shape.

3. The farmer measures the lengths of the sides of the garden. Then, he has to add them together to figure out how much fencing he will need.

"Painting a Room" Response (page 61)

1. D. a couple of hours later

2. Joey's mom has him take the measurements for the walls in his room and pick the paint color and supplies. She is also going to have him clean his room and move and cover his furniture.

3. Joey realizes that painting a room is a lot of work.

Let's Compare! How Big Is the Room? (page 62)

9 + 8 + 9 + 8 = 34 feet per wall

34 × 4 = 136 feet total

Understanding Perimeter

Mathematics Texts

	Lesson Steps	Teacher Think Alouds
Ready, Set, Predict!	• Provide the text to students and display a larger version. Have them share their observations about the diagrams that accompany the text with partners. • Have students discuss the following prompt: *I think the author will use high-level vocabulary in this passage because _____.*	"When I look at this text, I notice that it looks a lot like our math book. I see diagrams that show measurements, so I can relate this text to the pages I see in a math book."
Go!	• Allow time for students to read the text independently. Encourage them to use pencils to circle words they find tricky. • Read the text aloud to students. Model fluent reading. • Divide students into small groups. Have them read the text together. For additional rereading opportunities to help build fluency, see page 124.	"Watch how I read the part with the numbers. It sounds like steps need to be followed."
Reread to Clarify	• Tell students to reread the text with partners and box any words or ideas they want to clarify. Provide prompts to assist students who are hesitant such as *I don't get the part where _____, so I _____.* • Have students return to the text and underline the definitions of perimeter. Discuss real-life applications that would require knowing perimeter.	"Now that I know what *perimeter* is, I think about things in my own life that have perimeter. For example, our classroom has a perimeter."
Reread to Question	• Divide students into pairs. Ask them to reread the text to question. Have one student quiz his or her partner about perimeter. Then, have the pair switch roles. • Have students respond to the question and prompts on page 58.	
Reread to Summarize and Respond	• Tell students to reread the text to summarize. Help students summarize the steps to calculate perimeter. Then, work together with students to measure the sides of the classroom. As a class, figure out the perimeter of the classroom. • Review the close reading strategies with students by singing the song on page 128.	

*Note: For more tips, engagement strategies, and fluency options to include in this lesson, see pages 122–128.

Understanding Perimeter

Perimeter is the total distance around the outside of a two-dimensional shape. To find the perimeter of an object, follow these two steps:

1. Measure each side.

5 ft.

3 ft.   3 ft.

5 ft.

2. Add together all of the measurements.
   5 ft. + 3 ft. + 5 ft. + 3 ft. = 16 ft.

Real-Life Application

A farmer wants to build a fence around his garden. How much wood will he need? He will need to figure out the perimeter.

6 ft. + 10 ft. + 6 ft. + 10 ft. = 32 ft.

He will need 32 feet of fencing.

10 ft.

6 ft.   garden   6 ft.

10 ft.

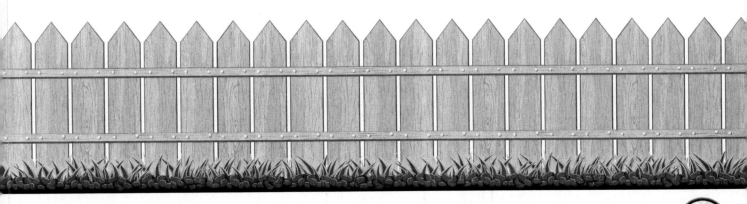

"Understanding Perimeter" Response

Directions: Reread the text on page 57 to answer each question.

1. What does the farmer want to figure out?

   Ⓐ The shape of his garden.   Ⓒ The area of his garden.

   Ⓑ The distance around the   Ⓓ The length of one side of
      sides of his garden.   his garden.

2. Why do you add the lengths of all the sides to find the perimeter
   of a shape?

   _____

   _____

   _____

   _____

   _____

3. Describe how the farmer will find the perimeter of his garden.

   _____

   _____

   _____

   _____

   _____

Fiction Text Teacher Notes
Painting a Room

	Lesson Steps	Teacher Think Alouds
Ready, Set, Predict!	• Provide students with the text and display a larger version. • Have students preview the text and make predictions with partners using the following: *I think _____ will happen because _____.*	"The title of a story is often a preview of what will happen in the text. I think a room will get painted in this story because of the title."
Go!	• Allow students to read through the text independently. Provide prompts to students to box words they do not know such as *Find the most interesting word* and *Find the longest word*. • Read the text aloud to students. Model reading the sentences in quotation marks using the vocal expressions for Joey and his mom. • Discuss the sequence of events in the story and how one event leads to another.	"I notice that Joey wanting to paint borders in his room leads to a chain of events in the story. He then has to measure his room, purchase supplies and paint, and clean his room. As I read about these events, I think about how one event causes another event."
Reread to Clarify	• Ask students to reread the text in small groups and circle words and sentences they want to clarify. Provide prompts to assist them with strategies for figuring out words and sentences they circle: *I don't make a picture in my head in the part about _____, so I _____.* • Have students return to the text and underline sentences that describe the work that must be done in order to paint a room.	"I don't make a picture in my head in the part about *500 shades of green*, so I talk with my group. They remind me that when I go to the paint store, there are all the paint samples along the wall of the paint department."
Reread to Question	• Pair students. Tell them to reread the text to ask and answer questions about it. Have one partner ask questions about Joey, and the other partner try to answer the questions. Then, have them switch roles. • Have students respond to the question and prompts on page 61.	
Reread to Summarize and Respond	• Tell students to reread the text to summarize by acting out important events. Invite partners to take turns acting out and guessing the events. • Review the close reading strategies with students by singing the song on page 128.	

*Note: For more tips, engagement strategies, and fluency options to include in this lesson, see pages 122–128.

Painting a Room

Adapted from a piece by Sharon Coan

"Mom, I'm sick of my room. It's so boring. It's been the same color since I was born. Can you paint a border around the walls today? Then my room will look extra cool!" whined Joey.

"Well, dear. I agree that your room needs painting. But, I think you are old enough to help with a lot of the work. While I'm getting ready, you need to measure the length of each wall and the height of the ceiling," smiled Mrs. Smith. She was thinking, "He's going to be surprised when he sees that it isn't such an easy job." That's how a Saturday morning began in the Smith family household.

Joey got his dad to help him with the measuring when he found out that it was hard for one person to do. Joey discovered that each wall was 9 feet (2.74 meters) long and the ceiling was 8 feet (2.44 meters) high. He wrote the dimensions of the room on a sheet of paper. Soon, Joey and his mom were off to the home-improvement store. On the way, Joey's mom casually asked him what color he wanted to paint the border. "I was thinking of green," Joey replied confidently.

At the store, Joey stood in awe of all the different colors of paint. There must have been 500 shades of green alone. "Just show me which shade of green you want, Joey," his mom said with a grin on her face.

A couple of hours later, having decided on the color of paint, the amount of paint, and the painting tools needed, Joey and his mom headed home.

In the car, Joey spoke in a small voice, "Mom, I'm pretty worn out today with all that decision making. Do you think we can paint next Saturday?"

"Sure, Joey. That will give you all week to get your room cleaned, your furniture moved, and covers over everything so paint won't get on your furniture," his mom replied.

Joey just groaned, "Maybe this wasn't such a bright idea."

"Painting a Room" Response

Directions: Reread the story on page 60 to answer each question.

1. What phrase did the author use to show that Joey and his mom spent a long time at the home-improvement store?

   Ⓐ Joey stood in awe.   Ⓒ Joey replied confidently.

   Ⓑ He wrote the dimensions.   Ⓓ a couple of hours later

2. Describe how Joey's mom involved him in preparing to paint his room.

   _____

   _____

   _____

   _____

   _____

   _____

3. Why does Joey state, *Maybe this wasn't such a bright idea*?

   _____

   _____

   _____

   _____

   _____

Name: _____   **Date:** _____

How Big Is the Room?

Directions: Use the measurements in "Painting a Room" and the directions on figuring out perimeter in "Understanding Perimeter" to figure out the perimeter of each wall in Joey's room.

Hint: His walls are rectangles. There are four of them.

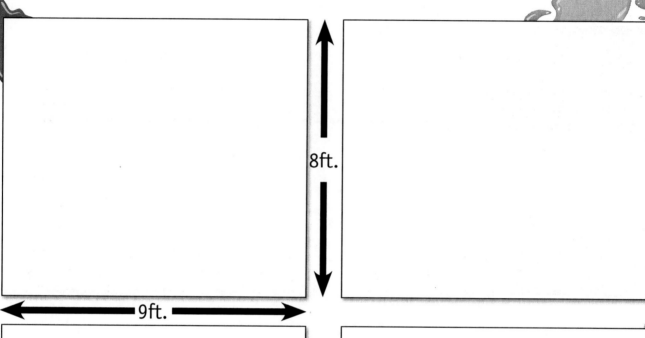

8ft.

9ft.

Perimeter of each wall = _____

Total perimeter of all of the walls = _____

#51359—Close Reading with Paired Texts   © Shell Education

Thinking About Measurement!

Directions: Choose at least two of these activities to complete.

Radical Reading

Reread "Understanding Perimeter" in your best teacher voice. Then, read it in your best student voice.

Fun Fluency

Practice reading "Painting a Room" using different voices for Joey and his mom. Record yourself reading the text. Play your recording for a classmate.

Wonderful Words

Fold a sheet of paper into four sections. Label each section with the name of a color. Make lists of as many shades of each color as you can think of. When you cannot think of any more, ask friends to add to your list.

Wacky Writing

Work with a friend to rewrite "Painting a Room" as a reader's theater script. You may have to add some lines for a narrator. Practice reading your new script until it sounds fluent. Perform your reader's theater for the class.

Storms

Theme Summary

Some weather can be destructive. Students will enjoy a fiction text written in a diary format based on *The Wizard of Oz* and enjoy learning facts about tornados and hurricanes in the nonfiction piece. Students will either be ready to run away from or chase storms after reading this text pair!

Answer Key

"Super Storms" Response (page 67)

1. D. flooding

2. Due to the Earth's rotation, clouds rush to the eye, but it remains calm because it does not have any clouds or wind.

3. A hurricane that reaches land can cause large waves, which then causes flooding. High winds, lightning, and rain are also possible.

"Dear Diary" Response (page 70)

1. B. She is upset that her flower beds are ruined.

2. The storm influences the story because the tornado causes the house to be lifted up.

3. Because Dorothy hits her head, she is not sure which events really happen and which do not.

Let's Compare! Fact or Fiction? (page 71)

Students may underline the following parts: *clouds whirled, house was lifted up from the storm, We could see lightning and rain*, and *winds began to blow furiously*. Students may cross out the following parts: *angry green color* and *I saw Mrs. Gultch on her bicycle in the air!*

Students' diary entries will vary.

Standards

➡ Describe characters in a story (e.g., their traits, motivations, or feelings) and explain how their actions contribute to the sequence of events.

➡ Describe the relationship between a series of historical events, scientific ideas or concepts, or steps in technical procedures in a text, using language that pertains to time, sequence, and cause/effect.

➡ Know a variety of natural hazards result from natural processes. Know that humans cannot eliminate natural hazards but can take steps to reduce their impact.

Materials

➡ *Super Storms* (pages 66–67)

➡ *"Super Storms" Response* (page 67)

➡ *Dear Diary* (page 69)

➡ *"Dear Diary" Response* (page 70)

➡ *Let's Compare! Fact or Fiction?* (page 71)

➡ *Thinking About Storms!* (page 72)

➡ pencils

➡ index cards

➡ crayons

➡ drawing paper

Comparing the Texts

After students complete the lessons for each text, have them work in pairs or groups to reread both texts and complete the *Let's Compare! Fact or Fiction?* activity page (page 71). Finally, students can work to complete the *Thinking About Storms!* matrix (page 72). The activities allow students to work on the important literacy skills of reading, writing, vocabulary, and fluency.

Super Storms

		Lesson Steps	Teacher Think Alouds
	Ready, Set, Predict!	• Provide students with the text and display a larger version. Identify and discuss the subheadings with students. • Ask partners to respond to the following: *I think the author wrote this text to* (e.g., *inform, persuade, entertain*) _____ *because* _____.	"I think the author wrote this text to inform because two types of storms are listed in the subheadings. I think I am going to learn about tornadoes and hurricanes."
	Go!	• Have students read the text independently. Encourage them to place smiley faces next to words with the most vowels. • Read the text aloud to students. Model fluent reading. Discuss with students the informational nature of this text. **Note:** You may wish to read the text to them in the voice of a reporter to help convey that the information is nonfiction.	"When I read the word *rotating* in the phrase *rotating storm systems*, I notice that I pronounce the *a* as a short vowel. When I reread the word, I use the long *a* sound. Now the word sounds right."
	Reread to Clarify	• Ask students to reread the text and circle words they want to clarify. Ask them to work with partners to figure out strategies to clarify the words they circle. • Invite students to return to the text and underline the sentence that best describes each type of storm. Have them share their sentences with partners.	
	Reread to Question	• Provide each student with two index cards. Ask students to reread the text and write questions about tornadoes or hurricanes on one of their cards. Collect the cards. On the other card, have students write *tornadoes* on one side and *hurricanes* on the other. Ask each question to the class and tell students to hold up the side of the card that answers it. • Have students respond to the question and prompts on page 67.	
	Reread to Summarize and Respond	• Tell students to reread the text to summarize by underlining ways the two storms are the same with one color crayon and ways they are different with another color. • Review the close reading strategies with students by singing the song on page 128.	"I read that the storms are different in many ways, so I pay close attention to the ways they are different as I read."

*****Note:** For more tips, engagement strategies, and fluency options to include in this lesson, see pages 122–128.

Super Storms

There are many different types of storms, but two of the most powerful are tornadoes and hurricanes. They are different in many ways, but can both be very destructive.

Tornadoes

A tornado is a bad storm that acts like a huge vacuum. It moves at a high speed. It can go as fast as 31 miles (50 kilometers) per hour. Tornadoes pick up everything in their paths and drop them far away. Even heavy items like trucks are no match for a tornado's strength.

Tornadoes start as thunderstorms over land. These huge storms can form supercells, which start to turn. The supercells are huge rainstorms that can have thunder and lightning. They can cause hail and strong winds. Strong winds blow around the storm. The air inside the clouds starts to spin. The spinning winds can touch the ground. Once that happens, it is a tornado.

Hurricanes

Each year, hurricanes cause more damage than all other storms combined. Hurricanes start as tropical storms over warm water in late summer or fall. They are rotating storm systems with strong winds and heavy rains. Hurricanes have wind speeds of over 75 miles (120 kilometers) per hour.

The center of a hurricane is called the eye. Clouds rush toward it. But they start to spin due to Earth's rotation. As a result, the eye stays calm. It has no clouds and no wind.

Super Storms (cont)

As soon as hurricanes reach land, they lose much of their power. There can still be a lot of damage on the land, though. A hurricane causes large waves which crash onto shore. This causes flooding. High winds blow, lightning flashes, and rain pours. A hurricane can cause millions of dollars in damage.

"Super Storms" Response

Directions: Reread the text on pages 66–67 to answer each question.

1. Which of the following is **not** mentioned as an effect of a tornado?

   Ⓐ hail   Ⓒ strong wind

   Ⓑ spinning air   Ⓓ flooding

2. How does the eye of the hurricane remain calm even though it is the center of the hurricane?

_____

_____

_____

_____

3. Describe the effects of a hurricane once it reaches land.

_____

_____

_____

_____

Fiction Text Teacher Notes
Dear Diary

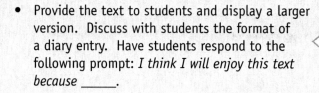

	Lesson Steps	Teacher Think Alouds
Ready, Set, Predict! 	• Provide the text to students and display a larger version. Discuss with students the format of a diary entry. Have students respond to the following prompt: *I think I will enjoy this text because _____*.	"I think I will enjoy this text because it is written in a diary format. We don't read many texts in this format, so I think it will be fun to read."
Go! 	• Allow time for students to read through the text independently. Encourage them to put smiley faces next to fun words as they read the text. • Read the text aloud to students. Model fluent reading. Have students return to the text and highlight all the exclamation marks. • Have partners reread the text. Encourage them to read sentences that have exclamation marks with excitement and surprise.	"Notice how I use a lot of excitement and surprise in my voice when I read the sentence *Then, our house was lifted up in the storm!* "
Reread to Clarify 	• Ask small groups to reread the text and circle words they want to clarify. Provide time for them to work together to find strategies for the words they circle. • Have students box the following words in the text: *enormous* and *furiously*. Tell them to underline the parts in surrounding sentences that help them identify the meanings of these words.	"I don't know the meaning of *enormous*, but the next sentence describes two small tornadoes. The tornado in the story is described as enormous and is nothing like the small ones. The sentence after that describes the tornado as really big, so I figure that *enormous* must mean 'really big.'"
Reread to Question	• Divide the class into two groups and have all students reread the text to ask and answer questions. Assign one group to write questions about the dream before the tornado and the other group to write questions about the dream after the tornado. Tell the groups to exchange questions. Ask groups to answer the questions they receive. • Have students respond to the question and prompts on page 70.	
Reread to Summarize and Respond 	• Provide students with drawing paper that has been folded into three sections. Have them reread the text to summarize by illustrating the dream before the tornado, during the tornado, and after the tornado. Students can share their illustrations with each other.	

*Note: For more tips, engagement strategies, and fluency options to include in this lesson, see pages 122–128.

Dear Diary

Dear Diary,

I had a very scary dream last night! I dreamt that my family and I were caught in an enormous tornado. I have seen two small tornadoes in real life, but this one was nothing like the ones I've experienced before. This one was really big—and kind of strange, too.

It all started on a beautiful Saturday morning. My dog, Toto, and I were playing and minding our own business. But mean Mrs. Gultch came by and said that Toto had ruined her flower beds! She brought the sheriff. They wanted to take Toto away. We ran to hide, but the storm came up fast. We didn't expect it! We ran for cover back home, but I hit my head and couldn't make it to the storm cellar.

Clouds whirled in an angry green color, and winds began to blow furiously around us. We could see lightning and rain. The storm crept closer and closer to our home. We could see the damage it was causing along its path. We were frozen with fear.

Then, our house was lifted up in the storm! The tornado whirled around us. I even think I saw Mrs. Gultch on her bicycle in the air! Maybe I just imagined her because of the bump on my head, but it sure seemed real!

Next, a lot of strange stuff happened that I don't really remember, but I think there was something about a tin man and a scarecrow, and there may have been some flying monkeys. Weird, right? But before I knew it, I was waking up in my room. It must have all been a bad dream. Even though it was just a dream, it still felt very real and very scary. I certainly don't want to ever experience that again in a dream or in real life!

It's odd, though. I have a nagging desire to wear red shoes.

Dorothy

"Dear Diary" Response

Directions: Reread the diary entry on page 69 to answer each question.

1. What can you tell about Mrs. Gultch from reading this text?

   Ⓐ She is a witch.   ⓒ She is a sheriff.

   Ⓑ She is upset that her flower   Ⓓ She likes dogs.
       beds are ruined.

2. How does the storm influence the story? Give an example from
   the text.

   _____

   _____

   _____

   _____

   _____

3. How does Dorothy bumping her head affect what happens in the story?

   _____

   _____

   _____

   _____

   _____

Let's Compare!

Fact or Fiction?

Directions: Read the excerpt about the tornado from "Dear Diary" below. Use what you learned in "Super Storms" to underline the parts of the excerpt that accurately describe the tornado. Draw lines through the parts that are made up.

Excerpt from "Dear Diary"

Clouds whirled in an angry green color, and winds began to blow furiously around us. We could see lightning and rain. The storm crept closer and closer to our home. We could see the damage it was causing along its path. We were frozen with fear.

Then, our house was lifted up in the storm! The tornado whirled around us. I even think I saw Mrs. Gultch on her bicycle in the air! Maybe I just imagined her because of the bump on my head, but it sure seemed real!

• •

Directions: Write a diary entry about a hurricane. The diary entry can be real or a dream.

_____

_____

_____

_____

_____

_____

_____

_____

Thinking About Storms!

Science Texts

Directions: Choose at least two of these activities to complete.

Radical Reading

Read "Super Storms" with a partner. One person can read about tornadoes. The other person can read about hurricanes. After you have practiced several times and can read it fluently, record yourselves reading it and listen to your recording.

Fun Fluency

Practice reading "Dear Diary" with a surprised expression in your voice. Once you can read it fluently, perform it for a small group or another class.

Wonderful Words

Make a list of weather words. Reread the list and circle any words that can be used to describe storms. Choose three of the words and include them in a short paragraph about weather in the form of a weather report. Then, present your weather report to a partner.

Wacky Writing

Reread the details about Mrs. Gultch from "Dear Diary." Write a diary entry from her perspective. Make sure the diary entry portrays her correctly based on what you've read about her.

Life Cycles

Theme Summary

All living things go through stages of growth and development, but each in its own way. Students will learn about the stages of a butterfly's life by reading a fable and a nonfiction text in this text pair. Your students will be ready to soar after working with these texts!

Standards

➡ Recount stories, including fables, folktales, and myths from diverse cultures; determine the central message, lesson, or moral and explain how it is conveyed through key details in the text.

➡ Describe the logical connection between particular sentences and paragraphs in a text.

➡ Know that plants and animals progress through life cycles of birth, growth and development, reproduction, and death; the details of these life cycles are different for different organisms.

Materials

➡ *A Butterfly's Life* (page 75)

➡ *"A Butterfly's Life" Response* (page 76)

➡ *The Ant and the Chrysalis* (page 78)

➡ *"The Ant and the Chrysalis" Response* (page 79)

➡ *Let's Compare! Which Stage?* (page 80)

➡ *Thinking About Life Cycles!* (page 81)

➡ pencils

➡ drawing paper

➡ crayons, including black and orange

➡ index cards

Comparing the Texts

After students complete the lessons for each text, have them work in pairs or groups to reread both texts and complete the *Let's Compare! Which Stage?* activity page (page 80). Finally, students can work to complete the *Thinking About Life Cycles!* matrix (page 81). The activities allow students to work on the important literacy skills of reading, writing, vocabulary, and fluency.

Answer Key

"A Butterfly's Life" Response (page 76)

1. D. pupa stage

2. Some butterflies stay inside the chrysalis for a couple of weeks and some stay inside the chrysalis for a couple of months.

3. Butterflies need their wings to fly in order to find good places to lay eggs.

"The Ant and the Chrysalis" Response (page 79)

1. C. The chrysalis could not talk.

2. The ant feels sorry for the chrysalis and pities it. The ant boasts of all the things it could do that the chrysalis could not.

3. The butterfly flies away and does not talk to the ant again.

Let's Compare! Which Stage? (page 80)

Students may include the following for the first excerpt: The excerpt is talking about the third process in a butterfly's life cycle. The lines *Then, the caterpillar spins a chrysalis* and *Most caterpillars stay inside the chrysalis for a couple of weeks* from "A Butterfly's Life" help support this.

Students may include the following for the second excerpt: The excerpt is talking about the fourth and final stage in a butterfly's life cycle. The lines *When the caterpillar emerges, it has become a beautiful butterfly* and *It has wings that it uses to fly* from "A Butterfly's Life" help support this.

Nonfiction Text Teacher Notes
A Butterfly's Life

	Lesson Steps	Teacher Think Alouds
Ready, Set, Predict!	• Distribute the text to students and display a larger version. • Invite students to make predictions with partners using the following: *I think I will learn _____ because _____.*	
 **Go!**	• Allow time for students to read the text independently. Have them think about the content. • Read the text aloud to students. Model fluent reading. • Have students reread the text in small groups and put asterisks (*) next to the names of each stage of a butterfly's life cycle.	"Notice how I self-correct. I read the word *lava*, but that doesn't sound right because we are not reading about volcanoes. I look more closely at the word and realize it is *larva*, which makes more sense."
 **Reread to Clarify**	• Ask students to reread the text with partners and circle words they want to clarify. Have partners discuss the strategies they used to clarify the words using the following: *I make a picture in my head in the part about _____.* • Have students reread each stage of a butterfly's life and underline important characteristics of that stage. Encourage students to switch crayon colors for each stage.	"I make a picture in my head in the part about some chrysalis being underground. I think about a hole in the ground with a chrysalis in it."
 **Reread to Question**	• Tell students to reread the text to question. Divide them into groups of four and have each student in a group choose a different stage of the life cycle to write a question about. • Provide time for the students in the group to ask and answer the questions. • Have students respond to the question and prompts on page 76.	
Reread to Summarize and Respond	• Provide students with drawing paper. Have them reread the text to summarize by drawing sequence maps that show the stages described in the text. Tell them to illustrate each stage and write one or two sentences about it. Ask partners to share their maps with one another.	"When I read about stages, I think about sequence. A way to help me understand this is to draw the sequence being described by the words such as *a chrysalis usually hangs from under a branch or leaf.*"

*Note: For more tips, engagement strategies, and fluency options to include in this lesson, see pages 122–128.

A Butterfly's Life

Every living thing goes through stages in its life. A butterfly is no different.

First, a butterfly lays an egg on a leaf. A butterfly egg is very small. It can be as small as the period at the end of this sentence. This is called the larva stage.

Next, a caterpillar hatches out of the egg. The leaf becomes food for the caterpillar when it hatches from the egg. Caterpillars feed and grow during this time. They grow up to 100 times their size and shed their skin four or five times as they grow.

Then, the caterpillar spins a chrysalis. This is also called the pupa stage. The chrysalis usually hangs from under a branch or leaf. Sometimes the chrysalis is underground. Most caterpillars stay inside the chrysalises for a couple of weeks, but some species can stay in for a couple of months.

When the caterpillar emerges, it has become a beautiful butterfly. A butterfly has six legs and two antennae. It has wings that it uses to fly. The wings are very important! A butterfly must fly to find a good place to lay eggs. Then, the cycle can begin again.

"A Butterfly's Life" Response

Directions: Reread the text on page 75 to answer each question.

1. What is the chrysalis stage also known as?

   Ⓐ butterfly stage   Ⓒ caterpillar stage

   Ⓑ larva stage   Ⓓ pupa stage

2. Describe the differences between how long caterpillars can stay inside the chrysalises.

   _____

   _____

   _____

   _____

3. Why are a butterfly's wings important to the life cycle?

   _____

   _____

   _____

   _____

Fiction Text Teacher Notes
The Ant and the Chrysalis

Lesson Steps	Teacher Think Alouds

Ready, Set, Predict!
- Read the title of the text to students. Have them predict what the story will be about.
- Provide the text to students and display a larger version. Ask partners to respond to the following: *I know _____ is about this topic.*

Go!
- Have students independently read the text.
- Read the text aloud to students. Model expressive reading.
- Tell students to underline the ant's quotations with black crayons and the butterfly's quotations with orange crayons. Have partners reread the text. Encourage them to use different voices for the ant and the butterfly.

"Notice how I read what the ant says to the butterfly with a prideful and boastful voice."

Reread to Clarify
- Ask students to reread the text and circle words they have difficulty with. Have partners discuss strategies for understanding those words.
- Tell students to box the sentence *What a sad fate is yours!* Then, have them underline clues the author provides that help us understand what the boxed sentence means.

"I don't understand the word *metamorphosis*, so I look it up in the dictionary and find out that it is 'the change a caterpillar makes to become a butterfly.'"

Reread to Question
- Provide index cards to students. Ask partners to reread the text and write questions on the cards that can be answered with the words *ant* or *butterfly*. Collect the questions.
- Provide more index cards to students. Have them write *ant* on one side and *butterfly* on the other. Ask the questions that students came up with. Students should hold up their index cards, showing the answer as either ant or butterfly.
- Have students respond to the question and prompts on page 79.

"Which insect in the story feels sorry for the chrysalis?"

Reread to Summarize and Respond
- Tell students to reread the text to summarize. Ask them to focus on the moral at the end of the fable. Have students return to the text and put asterisks (*) next to key details that help explain the moral. Invite students to share their marked parts with partners.

"When I read the moral at the end of the fable, I look for evidence in the text that supports it such as the line *Poor, pitiful animal! What a sad fate is yours!*"

*Note: For more tips, engagement strategies, and fluency options to include in this lesson, see pages 122–128.

The Ant and the Chrysalis

An ant nimbly running about in the sunshine in search of food came across a chrysalis that was very near its time of metamorphosis. The chrysalis moved its tail and attracted the attention of the ant, who then saw for the first time that it was alive. "Poor, pitiful animal! What a sad fate is yours! While I can run hither and thither at my pleasure, you lie imprisoned here in your shell, with power only to move a joint or two of your scaly tail." The chrysalis heard all this, but it did not try to make any reply.

A few days later, when the ant passed that way again, nothing but the shell remained. Wondering what had happened to its contents, the ant felt itself suddenly fanned by the gorgeous wings of a beautiful butterfly. "Behold in me your much-pitied friend! Boast now of your powers to run and climb! But it will be difficult for me to listen," said the butterfly. For after he said this, the butterfly rose in the air, borne along and aloft on the summer breeze, and was soon lost to the sight of the ant forever.

The moral of this fable is, "Appearances are deceptive."

Name: _____ **Date:** _____

"The Ant and the Chrysalis" Response

Directions: Reread the story on page 78 to answer each question.

1. Why did the chrysalis **not** reply to the ant at the beginning of the story?

   (A) It did not like the ant.   (C) The chrysalis could not talk.

   (B) It did not move.   (D) The ant was rude.

2. How does the ant feel about the chrysalis?

   _____

   _____

   _____

3. Why does the butterfly say, *But it will be difficult for me to listen?*

   _____

   _____

   _____

   _____

Let's Compare!

Which Stage?

Science Texts

Directions: Read the excerpts from "The Ant and the Chrysalis." Use evidence from "A Butterfly's Life" to describe the stages in the life cycle.

The Ant and the Chrysalis	A Butterfly's Life
An ant nimbly running about in the sunshine in search of food came across a chrysalis that was very near its time of metamorphosis. The chrysalis moved its tail and attracted the attention of the ant, who then saw for the first time that it was alive. "Poor, pitiful animal! What a sad fate is yours! While I can run hither and thither at my pleasure, you lie imprisoned here in your shell, with power only to move a joint or two of your scaly tail." The chrysalis heard all this, but it did not try to make any reply.	
Wondering what had happened to its contents, the ant felt itself suddenly fanned by the gorgeous wings of a beautiful butterfly. "Behold in me your much-pitied friend! Boast now of your powers to run and climb! But it will be difficult for me to listen," said the butterfly. For after he said this, the butterfly rose in the air, borne along and aloft on the summer breeze, and was soon lost to the sight of the ant forever.	

Thinking About Life Cycles!

Directions: Choose at least two of these activities to complete.

Radical Reading

Reread "A Butterfly's Life." Underline the transition words (for example, *first, next, then*) and phrases in the text. Make a list of other transition words that show sequence.

Fun Fluency

Reread "The Ant and the Chrysalis" with two other people. One person can read the ant's lines. A second person can read the butterfly's lines. The third person can read all the remaining lines. Practice until you can read the story fluently. Perform your version for another class.

Wonderful Words

Write the word *metamorphosis* at the top of a sheet of paper. Write as many words as you can using the letters in *metamorphosis*. Assign yourself two points for two-letter words, three points for three-letter words, etc. Total up your points. Try to get at least 20 points.

Wacky Writing

Write a fable about the life cycle of another animal that you are familiar with (for example, *frog, bird*). Be sure to include a lesson or a moral. Share your fable with a partner.

Gravity

Theme Summary

The old saying is, "What goes up, must come down." The thing about this old saying is that it is not just a saying; it is a law of nature. In this text pair, students will learn more about gravity and the real-life effects of gravity. This text pair is sure to keep your students grounded!

Answer Key

"Understanding Gravity" Response (page 85)

1. D. It is one of the strongest forces around.

2. Gravity holds us to the ground. Otherwise, we would float up into space.

3. Gravity keeps the moon going around Earth.

"A Skateboard Trick" Response (page 88)

1. B. He learns a skateboard trick.

2. Student answers will vary but may include: *Shawn has fallen out of a tree and broke a bone* or *Shawn has fallen off his bunk bed*.

3. Mom knows Shawn will try some more skateboard tricks. If he falls, gravity will pull him to the ground and the helmet will protect his head.

Let's Compare! A Scientific Definition (page 89)

Students' responses will vary, but students may underline some of the following: *Gravity is a force that pulls one physical body to another body; uses its gravity to pull me . . .down;* and *Gravity brought you back to the grass below.*

Standards

➠ Describe characters in a story (e.g., their traits, motivations, or feelings) and explain how their actions contribute to the sequence of events.

➠ Determine the meaning of general academic and domain-specific words and phrases in a text relevant to a grade 3 topic or subject area.

➠ Know that the Earth's gravity pulls any object toward it without touching it.

Materials

➠ *Understanding Gravity* (page 84)

➠ *"Understanding Gravity" Response* (page 85)

➠ *A Skateboard Trick* (pages 87–88)

➠ *"A Skateboard Trick" Response* (page 88)

➠ *Let's Compare! A Scientific Definition* (page 89)

➠ *Thinking About Gravity!* (page 90)

➠ pencils

➠ crayons

➠ writing paper

Comparing the Texts

After students complete the lessons for each text, have them work in pairs or groups to reread both texts and complete the *Let's Compare! A Scientific Definition* activity page (page 89). Finally, students can work to complete the *Thinking About Gravity!* matrix (page 90). The activities allow students to work on the important literacy skills of reading, writing, vocabulary, and fluency.

Nonfiction Text Teacher Notes
Understanding Gravity

		Lesson Steps	Teacher Think Alouds
	Ready, Set, Predict!	• Provide the text to students and display a larger version. Have them quietly skim the text. • Have students turn to partners and respond to the following prompt: *I already know _____ about gravity.*	"My knowledge of this topic is limited. I have heard the word *gravity* before, but I don't really understand what it is. I think this text will teach me about gravity."
	Go!	• Allow students to read through the text independently. Have them put asterisks (*) next to words or ideas that are challenging to them. • Read the text aloud to students. Model fluent reading by pausing at commas and at the ends of sentences. • Have students use yellow crayons to highlight all the ending punctuation and commas.	"Notice how I pause at each comma when I read this sentence: *A force is a push, pull, or twist on one object based on the activity of another object.*"
	Reread to Clarify	• Tell students to reread the text and circle phrases or sentences they want to clarify. Allow time for partners to use strategies to clarify the words they circle. Provide prompts to assist students such as: *The sentence _____ is tricky, so I _____* (e.g., *reread, read on, study*). • Invite students to underline the sentence or phrase that best describes gravity.	"The sentence about gravity being *a force that attracts one physical body to another one* is tricky, so I keep reading and read that gravity keeps the moon going around Earth and that helps me better understand the phrase."
	Reread to Question	• Divide students into two groups. Have them reread the text to question. Have one group write questions about the first paragraph. Have the other group write questions about the second paragraph. Tell the groups to exchange the questions and then answer the questions they receive. • Have students respond to the question and prompts on page 85.	
	Reread to Summarize and Respond	• Tell students to reread the text to summarize. Ask students to hold out pencils or other non-breakable objects and drop them from chest height. Ask students to verbally share with partners what happens and how it relates to what they read about in the text.	

*Note: For more tips, engagement strategies, and fluency options to include in this lesson, see pages 122–128.

Understanding Gravity

Gravity is one of the strongest forces around. If it were a living thing, it would be a superhero! But it is not living. It is a force. A force is a push, pull, or twist on one object based on the activity of another object. Gravity is a force that attracts one physical body to another one. You cannot see gravity. You cannot touch it. But it makes the planets go around the sun. It keeps the moon going around Earth. And it keeps you grounded on Earth rather than floating up into space.

Try jumping as high as you can. No matter how high you jump, you come back down again. That is gravity. Everything that is not held up by another force comes down because of gravity. There is no way to avoid it. Gravity is like a law. It is a law of nature!

"Understanding Gravity" Response

Directions: Reread the text on page 84 to answer each question.

1. Why is gravity described as a superhero?

   (A) It is a law of nature.

   (B) There is no way to avoid it.

   (C) It is a force.

   (D) It is one of the strongest forces around.

2. What is one way gravity works on you every day?

   _____

   _____

   _____

   _____

   _____

3. How does gravity affect the moon?

   _____

   _____

   _____

   _____

   _____

Fiction Text Teacher Notes
A Skateboard Trick

	Lesson Steps	Teacher Think Alouds
Ready, Set, Predict!	• Provide the text to students and display a larger version. Have them review its format. • Have students turn to partners and discuss the following prompt: *I think I will enjoy this text because _____.*	"I think I will enjoy this text because it is a reader's theater script, and I love reading a text with other people."
Go!	• Invite students to read through the text independently. Encourage them to use pencils to place asterisks (*) next to words they are not familiar with. • Read the text to students. Be sure to change your voice for Mom and Shawn. Discuss how and why you make your voice sound different for the two characters. • Divide the class into two groups. One group can read Mom's lines and the other can read Shawn's lines. Read the text aloud with each group reading its part.	"When I read Shawn's lines, I make my voice excited to show how Shawn feels about doing an ollie. When I read Mom's lines, I make my voice sound happy and supportive to show how she feels toward her son's new accomplishments."
Reread to Clarify	• Have students reread the text and circle any words or ideas they think are tricky or confusing. Allow time for them to work with partners to discuss strategies they use to understand the words they circle. • Tell students to underline the parts that best describe Shawn's skateboard trick.	
Reread to Question	• Divide students into groups of four. Have them reread the text to question it. Have one pair within the group write questions about Mom. Have the other pair write questions about Shawn. The pairs can ask each other the questions they wrote. • Have students respond to the question and prompts on page 88.	
Reread to Summarize and Respond	• Ask students to reread the text to summarize by boxing sentences that show each character's feelings. • Invite partners to act out conversations between Mom and Shawn. They should express the feelings that they boxed.	"As I read the lines for each character, I read that Mom and Shawn have different feelings and motivations. I realize that Shawn feels excited because he learns how to ollie, and mom feels concerned about Shawn's understanding of the effects of gravity."

*Note: For more tips, engagement strategies, and fluency options to include in this lesson, see pages 122–128.

A Skateboard Trick

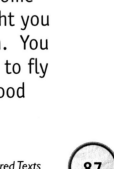

Shawn: Mom, Mom, I did it! I did an ollie!

Mom: Who's Ollie?

Shawn: Oh, Mom, you're funny. It's not a who, it's a what.

Mom: Okay, what's an ollie?

Shawn: It's a skateboard trick!

Mom: Cool! How do you do an ollie?

Shawn: You put one foot in the middle of the board and the other foot at the back of the board. Then, push the tail down so it smacks the ground and the board flies up.

Mom: Wow!

Shawn: That's not all. As the board flies up, you pull your knees to your chest. Then, you land with your knees bent.

Mom: That sounds impressive! But I hope you remember two things.

Shawn: What's that?

Mom: What goes up, must come down.

Shawn: What does that mean?

Mom: Just a friendly reminder from Gravity, an old friend of ours.

Shawn: Ha, ha. Okay, I get it. Gravity is a force that pulls one physical body to another body. So big old Earth uses its gravity to pull little old me back down to the ground whenever I go up, right? Okay, Mom, I get it.

Mom: Well, good. I thought you might. You and gravity have had some run-ins before. Remember climbing that tree? Gravity brought you back to the grass below long before you meant to come down. You had a cast for a few weeks after that! And when you wanted to fly off your bunk bed like Superman, there was gravity again. Good thing Daddy was there to catch you!

A Skateboard Trick (cont)

Shawn: Oh, don't remind me. Okay, so I know about gravity. But you said to remember two things. What else? Be careful, right?

Mom: Well, yes, be careful. But that wasn't the second thing I was going to say.

Shawn: Well then, what else should I remember?

Mom: Your helmet!

Shawn: Oh, you're a regular comedian, Mom.

• •

"A Skateboard Trick" Response

Directions: Reread the script on pages 87–88 to answer each question.

1. Why is Shawn so excited?

    Ⓐ He learns about gravity.   Ⓒ He learns school is hard.

    Ⓑ He learns a skateboard trick.   Ⓓ He learns to be careful.

2. Describe one other way Shawn experiences gravity.

_____

_____

3. Use evidence to tell why Shawn's mom reminds him to bring his helmet.

_____

_____

_____

Let's Compare!

A Scientific Definition

Directions: Underline phrases or sentences in the excerpt that give scientific explanations of gravity. Use what you learned from "Understanding Gravity" to help you.

A Skateboard Trick

Mom: That sounds impressive! But I hope you remember two things.

Shawn: What's that?

Mom: What goes up, must come down.

Shawn: What does that mean?

Mom: Just a friendly reminder from Gravity, an old friend of ours.

Shawn: Ha, ha. Okay, I get it. Gravity is a force that pulls one physical body to another body. So big old Earth uses its gravity to pull little old me back down to the ground whenever I go up, right? Okay, Mom, I get it.

Mom: Well, good. I thought you might. You and gravity have had some run-ins before. Remember climbing that tree? Gravity brought you back to the grass below long before you meant to come down. You had a cast for a few weeks after that! And when you wanted to fly off your bunk bed like Superman, there was gravity again. Good thing Daddy was there to catch you!

Shawn: Oh, don't remind me. Okay, so I know about gravity.

Thinking About Gravity!

Directions: Choose at least two of these activities to complete.

Radical Reading

Read "A Skateboard Trick" with a partner. Each of you should read one of the characters' roles. Practice until you can read it fluently. Then, perform it for a small group of friends.

Fun Fluency

Practice reading "A Skateboard Trick" by yourself. Use a mom voice for Mom's lines and a kid's voice for Shawn's lines. Practice until you can read it fluently. Then, record yourself reading it. Play your recording for a partner.

Wonderful Words

Skateboarding is a fun way to get exercise. Make a list of other activities that help you get exercise. Go back and circle the activities that can be affected by gravity.

Wacky Writing

Write a short story about what would happen if you woke up one day and there was no gravity here on Earth. What would happen to the people and all the things on our planet?

Unit 10 Overview
Veterans Day

Theme Summary

Most schools take Veterans Day off as a holiday, but how many students actually know the significance of this holiday? Students will learn about Veterans Day through a reader's theater script and a nonfiction text telling about why the holiday was created. This text pair will leave you and your students feeling patriotic!

Standards

➡ Ask and answer questions to demonstrate understanding of a text, referring explicitly to the text as the basis for the answers.

➡ Describe the relationship between a series of historical events, scientific ideas or concepts, or steps in technical procedures in a text, using language that pertains to time, sequence, and cause/effect.

➡ Understand the events and democratic values commemorated by major national holidays.

Materials

➡ *A Day to Remember* (page 93)

➡ *"A Day to Remember" Response* (page 94)

➡ *Honoring Veterans* (page 96)

➡ *"Honoring Veterans" Response* (page 97)

➡ *Let's Compare! A Day for Veterans* (page 98)

➡ *Thinking About Veterans Day!* (page 99)

➡ pencils

➡ yellow crayons

➡ writing paper

Comparing the Texts

After students complete the lessons for each text, have them work in pairs or groups to reread both texts and complete the *Let's Compare! A Day for Veterans* activity page (page 98). Finally, students can work to complete the *Thinking About Veterans Day!* matrix (page 99). The activities allow students to work on the important literacy skills of reading, writing, vocabulary, and fluency.

Answer Key

"A Day to Remember" Response (page 94)

1. C. creation

2. Two minutes of silence were observed to honor the dead veterans at the exact time of the cease-fire.

3. Veterans Day was established because people wanted to honor all veterans, not just those from World War I.

"Honoring Veterans" Response (page 97)

1. B. We wanted to honor all veterans.

2. The Tomb of the Unknown Soldier was created, and there are parades on Veterans Day.

3. Answers may include that the author feels that veterans should be honored.

Let's Compare! A Day for Veterans (page 98)

Student responses may include the following:
The First Armistice Day—*Veterans paraded, people attended church services, two minutes of silence were observed; The first Armistice Day was for World War 1.*
A Change in Name—*Veterans Day was originally called Armistice Day; Armistice Day was changed to Veterans Day.*
Celebrating in America—*President Eisenhower signed into law the establishment of Veterans Day. It is celebrated November 11 each year; Americans wanted to honor all veterans. We also have parades.*
Celebrating Around the World—*In England, the British Commonwealth celebrates Remembrance Sunday. Canada has Remembrance Day. France and Australia also honor the losses in both World War I and World War II on or near November 11.*

Nonfiction Text Teacher Notes
A Day to Remember

		Lesson Steps	Teacher Think Alouds
	Ready, Set, Predict!	• Provide the text to students and display a larger version. Allow them time to preview the text to predict what type of text it is. • Have students discuss the following prompt with partners: *I think the author will use high-level vocabulary in this passage because _____.*	
	Go!	• Allow time for students to read the text independently. • Read the text aloud to students as you model fluency and comma use. • Have students use yellow crayons to highlight commas in the text. • Ask students to practice reading the text while pausing at the commas with partners.	"Notice how I pause at the commas when I read this sentence: *At exactly 11:00 A.M., the time of the cease-fire, two minutes of silence were observed in honor of the dead veterans.*"
	Reread to Clarify	• Tell students to reread the text and underline words or sentences they want to clarify. Allow time for students to work with partners to share strategies they use to clarify. • Have students return to the text and box sentences that tell how Armistice Day relates to Veterans Day.	"I don't know what the words *cease-fire* mean, so I look up the word *cease* in the dictionary and find out that it means 'to stop or end.' I figure out that *cease-fire* means to stop the fighting."
	Reread to Question	• Write the following stem on the board: *Why _____?* Ask students to reread the text and write their own sentences using the stem. Pair students together and tell them to respond to one another's questions. • Have students respond to the question and prompts on page 94.	
	Reread to Summarize and Respond	• Provide students with paper and have them fold it in half. Tell them to reread the text to summarize by writing the countries named in the text on one side, and writing what the countries do to celebrate veterans on the other side.	"When I read about other countries that also celebrate a day for veterans, I try to make connections to how we celebrate veterans."

*Note: For more tips, engagement strategies, and fluency options to include in this lesson, see pages 122–128.

A Day to Remember

Social Studies Texts

Adapted from a piece by Suzanne Barchers

Veterans Day was originally called Armistice Day. It was held to celebrate the end to World War I. On the first Armistice Day, November 11, 1918, veterans paraded, and people attended church services. At exactly 11:00 A.M., the time of the cease-fire, two minutes of silence were observed in honor of the dead veterans.

After World War I, there were other wars. Veterans died in World War II and the Korean War. People wanted to honor all of the veterans who had served the country. On June 1, 1954, President Dwight D. Eisenhower signed into law the establishment of Veterans Day. It is celebrated November 11 each year.

Other countries have days set aside to honor their veterans, too. In England, the British Commonwealth celebrates Remembrance Sunday. Canada has Remembrance Day. France and Australia also honor the losses in both World War I and World War II on or near November 11. Having a special holiday helps us stop and remember the veterans who have died for our countries.

"A Day to Remember" Response

Directions: Reread the text on page 93 to answer each question.

1. What does the word *establishment* mean in the sentence below?

> President Dwight D. Eisenhower signed into law the establishment of Veterans Day.

Ⓐ honor   Ⓒ creation

Ⓑ service   Ⓓ attend

2. What was the significance of two minutes of silence at exactly 11:00 A.M. on the first Armistice Day?

_____

_____

_____

_____

_____

3. Why was Veterans Day established?

_____

_____

_____

_____

_____

Fiction Text Teacher Notes
Honoring Veterans

	Lesson Steps	Teacher Think Alouds
Ready, Set, Predict!	• Provide the text to students and display a larger version. Have partners predict what the text will be about using the following: *I think this text is about _____ because _____.*	"I can see that two readers are going to take turns reading lines of this text. Each person will read every other line until the last line."
Go!	• Provide time for students to read through the text. Encourage them to place asterisks (*) next to words they want to know more about. • Read the text aloud to students. Use two different voices so that students are able to distinguish the two parts of the script. • Discuss the rhyming structure of the reader's theater script with students. Have them return to the text and box the words that rhyme. • Divide the class into two groups. Assign each group one part of the reader's theater script. Read the text with each group reading its assigned part. Then switch roles.	
Reread to Clarify	• Have students reread the text with partners and circle any words or sentences they want to clarify using the following: *The word _____ is tricky, so I _____* (e.g., *sound it out, look for parts I know, reread, read on*). • Ask students to underline sentences in the text that clarify why Veterans Day was started.	"The word *cease* is tricky, so I look for parts I know. I recognize *ease* from the word *please*, so I am able to figure out how to pronounce the word."
Reread to Question	• Pair students, and assign each student a part. Ask students to reread the text and write questions that can be answered in the text for their parts. Have them ask each other their questions and then discuss the answers. • Have students respond to the question and prompts on page 97.	"When I write questions, I use the words: *who, what, where, why, when,* and *how* to help me."
Reread to Summarize and Respond	• Tell partners to reread the text to summarize by discussing the following: *Before I read this text, I thought _____. Now I realize _____.* • Review the close reading strategies with students by singing the song on page 128.	

*****Note:** For more tips, engagement strategies, and fluency options to include in this lesson, see pages 122–128.

Name: _____ Date: _____

Honoring Veterans

by Suzanne Barchers

Reader 1: The first Armistice Day was for World War I.

Reader 2: An armistice means that the fighting is done.

Reader 1: The fighting had stopped on this very day.

Reader 2: The battle was over. Our military forces had won.

Reader 1: Armistice Day was changed to Veterans Day.

Reader 2: The change came in 1954.

Reader 1: Americans wanted to honor all veterans . . .

Reader 2: At home or away in war.

Reader 1: The Tomb of the Unknown Soldier holds veterans.

Reader 2: It helps honor those who have died.

Reader 1: We also have parades and remember those people . . .

Reader 2: Who have served as protectors with pride.

Reader 1: Thank you to the veterans.

Reader 2: We all wish war would cease.

Reader 1: Thank you for your service . . .

Both: In helping work for peace.

"Honoring Veterans" Response

Directions: Reread the script on page 96 to answer each question.

1. Why was Armistice Day changed to Veterans Day?

     Ⓐ The fighting stopped.   Ⓒ We wanted to have parades.

     Ⓑ We wanted to honor   Ⓓ The veterans were protectors.
        all veterans.

2. What are two ways we honor veterans?

_____

_____

_____

_____

_____

3. What evidence is there for how the author feels about veterans?

_____

_____

_____

_____

_____

Social Studies Texts

Let's Compare!

A Day for Veterans

Directions: Use evidence from "Honoring Veterans" and "A Day to Remember" to write a few sentences that tell about each subheading below.

The First Armistice Day

_____

_____

_____

A Change in Name

_____

_____

_____

Celebrating in America

_____

_____

_____

Celebrating Around the World

_____

_____

_____

#51359—Close Reading with Paired Texts   © Shell Education

Name: _____ **Date:** _____

Thinking About Veterans Day!

Directions: Choose at least two of these activities to complete.

Radical Reading

Reread either "Honoring Veterans" or "A Day to Remember." Circle the word *veteran* every time it appears in the text. Reread the text with a friend and have the friend read the circled words while you read the rest of the text.

Fun Fluency

Practice reading the reader's theater "Honoring Veterans" with a partner until you can read it fluently. Record yourselves reading it. Play your recording for a veteran.

Wonderful Words

Make a list of words with *-ay* in them. List three-letter words in one column, four-letter words in another column, and five- or more letter words in another column.

Wacky Writing

Write a letter to a veteran to thank him or her for his or her service. Send or hand-deliver the letter to the veteran.

Unit 11 Overview
Susan B. Anthony

Theme Summary

Sometimes it is hard to believe there was a time before women and other minorities had a right to vote. Through this poem and nonfiction text, students will learn about Susan B. Anthony's courageous efforts to bring the vote to everyone. This text pair will have you and your students ready to go to the polls!

Answer Key

"Amazing American: Susan B. Anthony" Response (page 103)

1. A. They had meetings.

2. Answers may include: Women were not paid the same, they could not vote, and they could not own houses.

3. Susan B. Anthony fought for equal rights for African Americans, and she got to see an end to slavery during her lifetime.

"Vote!" Response (page 106)

1. A. We found a way!

2. The picture is included on the poem to help the reader visualize women fighting for their right to vote.

3. The last stanza states *Now every woman can vote!* In the first two stanzas, they want the right to vote, but can't.

Let's Compare! Suffrage (page 107)

Students may include the following lines from "Amazing American: Susan B. Anthony":

Before—*Long ago, men had more rights than women; Many people wanted women to have the right to vote.*

During—*People worked hard for suffrage; Susan and her friends marched in parades; They gave speeches and had meetings.*

After—*Women won the right to vote in 1920.*

Standards

➡ Refer to parts of poems when writing or speaking about a text, using terms such as stanza; describe how each successive part builds on earlier sections.

➡ Ask and answer questions to demonstrate understanding of a text, referring explicitly to the text as the basis for the answers.

➡ Understand how people over the last 200 years have continued to struggle to bring all groups in American society the liberties and equality promised in the basic principles of American democracy.

Materials

➡ *Amazing American: Susan B. Anthony* (page 102)

➡ *"Amazing American: Susan B. Anthony" Response* (page 103)

➡ *Vote!* (page 105)

➡ *"Vote!" Response* (page 106)

➡ *Let's Compare! Suffrage* (page 107)

➡ *Thinking About Susan B. Anthony!* (page 108)

➡ pencils

➡ index cards

➡ colored pencils or crayons

Comparing the Texts

After students complete the lessons for each text, have them work in pairs or groups to reread both texts and complete the *Let's Compare! Suffrage* activity page (page 107). Finally, students can work to complete the *Thinking About Susan B. Anthony!* matrix (page 108). The activities allow students to work on the important literacy skills of reading, writing, vocabulary, and fluency.

Amazing American: Susan B. Anthony

Lesson Steps	Teacher Think Alouds
Ready, Set, Predict! • Provide students with the text and display a larger version. Have them skim the text for interesting vocabulary. • Have students turn to partners and predict the author's purpose using the following: *I think the author wrote this to _____ because _____.*	"As I preview the text, I think to myself, 'Are there any words in the text I think are interesting, unusual, or words that I am not familiar with?'"
Go! • Tell students to independently read the text. Encourage them to place asterisks (*) next to words that are tricky. • Model fluent reading as you read the text aloud to students. Then, ask students to reread the text to practice their fluency. • Review how to read the numbers in the text as dates (years) rather than numerals.	"This text is about historical events, so when I see numbers in the text, I don't read them as numerals, but rather as years. So, *1906* would be read as nineteen-o-six."
Reread to Clarify • Have students reread the text and circle words they want to clarify. Provide stems to support students as they use reading strategies to clarify the words they circle: *I don't understand _____, so I _____.* • Review the title with students. Have them return to the text and underline words or sentences that clarify why Susan B. Anthony was an amazing American.	"I don't understand the word *suffrage*, so I go back and reread the sentence before that word is used. Now I see that *suffrage* must mean the right to vote."
Reread to Question • Write question words (e.g., *who, what*) on one side of index cards, one word per card. Distribute the cards to students. Have them reread the text and write questions that begin with the words on their cards. Collect the questions and redistribute them to small groups. Encourage groups to answer the questions. • Have students respond to the question and prompts on page 103.	
Reread to Summarize and Respond • Ask students to reread the text to summarize by marking it up with the following symbols: ! cool idea ? I wonder + main idea ☺ details • Invite students to share their marked up parts with partners.	

*Note: For more tips, engagement strategies, and fluency options to include in this lesson, see pages 122–128.

Amazing American: Susan B. Anthony

Adapted from a piece by Stephanie Kuligowski

Susan B. Anthony was a smart and strong woman. She believed all people are equal. Anthony was born on February 15, 1820. When Anthony grew up, she became a teacher in New York. She earned $110 a year. Male teachers earned about $400 a year. Anthony thought this was unfair. She wanted better pay for women.

Anthony wanted to change the world. She fought for the rights of women and African Americans. Anthony wanted to change the way people were treated. Long ago, men had more rights than women had. Women could not own a house. They could not vote. Many people wanted to change things for women. They wanted women to have the right to vote. This was called suffrage.

People worked hard for suffrage. Anthony and her friends marched in parades. They gave speeches and had meetings. They did not give up. They wanted women to have equal rights. Anthony was an activist. She took action to make her world a better place.

Anthony saw the end of slavery, but she never got to vote legally. She died in 1906. Women won the right to vote in 1920.

"Amazing American: Susan B. Anthony" Response

Directions: Reread the text on page 102 to answer each question.

1. What is one way people worked for suffrage?

   Ⓐ They had meetings.

   Ⓑ They wanted better pay for women.

   Ⓒ They became teachers.

   Ⓓ They could not own a house.

2. Describe at least one way men had more rights than women.

   _____

   _____

   _____

   _____

   _____

3. The text states *She took action to make her world a better place.* In what way did she get to see this?

   _____

   _____

   _____

Fiction Text Teacher Notes
Vote!

		Lesson Steps	Teacher Think Alouds
	Ready, Set, Predict!	• Provide students with the text and display a larger version. Ask them to determine if there is a rhyming pattern. • Ask students to respond to the following prompt with partners: *I think I will enjoy reading this text because _____.*	"When I see lines repeat over and over in a poem, I know I can usually read them in a regular rhythm. Knowing this will help me read the poem."
	Go!	• Tell students to silently read the text. • Read the poem aloud to students. Model fluent reading. • Ask students to underline lines that repeat in the poem with one color pencil and lines that are different using a different color pencil. • Divide students into three groups. Assign each group a stanza. Reread the poem with each group reading their stanzas.	"Since there are so many lines that repeat in this poem, the lines that are different in each stanza are important to emphasize. Listen to how I emphasize those lines as I read the poem."
	Reread to Clarify	• Tell students to reread the text and circle words they want to know. Ask partners to discuss strategies they use to clarify the words. • Have students reread the poem in pairs. Ask them to create hand motions to go along with the words. Then, invite partners to perform the poem for one another.	
	Reread to Question	• Distribute index cards to students. Ask them to reread the text and write questions about it on the cards. Collect the cards. Assign three corners of the classroom with numbers (1, 2, 3). Ask a question. Students must determine which stanza the question is answered in and go to that corner. Discuss the answers as a class. • Have students respond to the question and prompts on page 106.	
	Reread to Summarize and Respond	• Tell students to reread the text to summarize by writing one sentence for each stanza that retells what happens in the stanza. Have them write one additional sentence that summarizes how each of the previous sentences build on each other.	"As I read the poem, I try to put what is happening in it in my own words. In the first stanza, Susan B. Anthony wants the right to vote for herself."

*****Note:** For more tips, engagement strategies, and fluency options to include in this lesson, see pages 122–128.

Vote!

Vote, vote, vote!
Let Susan B. Anthony vote!
She has a right!
She has a say!
Vote, vote, vote!

Vote, vote, vote!
Let every woman vote!
She has a right!
She has a say!
Vote, vote, vote!

Vote, vote, vote!
Now every woman can vote!
She has a right!
We found a way!
So, vote, vote, vote!

"Vote!" Response

Directions: Reread the poem on page 105 to answer each question.

1. What line does the author include to show that women won the right to vote?

   Ⓐ We found a way!   © She has a say!

   Ⓑ She has a right!   Ⓓ Vote, vote, vote!

2. Why is there an image included with the poem?

   _____

   _____

   _____

   _____

   _____

3. How have women's rights to vote changed by the last stanza?

   _____

   _____

   _____

   _____

   _____

Let's Compare!

Suffrage

Directions: Reread both texts. Use information from "Amazing American: Susan B. Anthony" to write about what it was like before, during, and after the suffrage movement.

	Vote!	Amazing American: Susan B. Anthony
Before	Vote, vote, vote! Let Susan B. Anthony vote! She has a right! She has a say! Vote, vote, vote!	
During	Vote, vote, vote! Let every woman vote! She has a right! She has a say! Vote, vote, vote!	
After	Vote, vote, vote! Now every woman can vote! She has a right! We found a way! So, vote, vote, vote!	

Thinking About Susan B. Anthony!

Directions: Choose at least two of these activities to complete.

Radical Reading

Reread "Amazing American: Susan B. Anthony" and underline everything she did to help other people.

Fun Fluency

Read "Vote!" with a partner. Have one person read the lines that repeat. The other person can read the remaining lines. Then, switch roles. Record the reading as a jingle to encourage people to vote.

Wonderful Words

Make a list of words from "Amazing American: Susan B. Anthony" that describe Susan B. Anthony. Circle the words that also describe you. Add new words that you feel describe both of you.

Wacky Writing

Write another stanza for the poem "Vote!" that describes the things Susan B. Anthony did to try to help get women the vote. Use information from "Amazing American: Susan B. Anthony" to help you with details.

Recycling

Social Studies Texts

Theme Summary

There was a time when people threw soda cans in the trash can without even thinking about it. Thankfully, recycling trends are growing and now, most of us give a second thought as to where that soda can goes. Students will learn about a family who begins recycling and about recycling trends in this text pair. If they are not already recycling, they will probably go home and set up bins at their houses!

Standards

⟹ Describe characters in a story and explain how their actions contribute to the sequence of events.

⟹ Use information gained from illustrations and the words in a text to demonstrate understanding of the text.

⟹ Know advantages and disadvantages of recycling and reusing different types of materials.

Materials

⟹ *Recycling Trends* (page 111)

⟹ *"Recycling Trends" Response* (page 112)

⟹ *Over and Over Again* (page 114)

⟹ *"Over and Over Again" Response* (page 115)

⟹ *Let's Compare! You Really Should Recycle* (page 116)

⟹ *Thinking About Recycling!* (page 117)

⟹ pencils

⟹ writing paper

⟹ drawing paper

⟹ coloring supplies

⟹ index cards

Comparing the Texts

After students complete the lessons for each text, have them work in pairs or groups to reread both texts and complete the *Let's Compare! You Really Should Recycle* activity page (page 116). Finally, students can work to complete the *Thinking About Recycling!* matrix (page 117). The activities allow students to work on the important literacy skills of reading, writing, vocabulary, and fluency.

Answer Key

"Recycling Trends" Response (page 112)

1. B. 1990

2. The trend is that more aluminum cans are being recycled for each time period that is being reported until the year 1990.

3. Other items that can be recycled include plastic bottles, glass, paper, newspaper, and tin cans.

"Over and Over Again" Response (page 115)

1. D. wood

2. Ann learned about recycling at school, so she told her parents about it.

3. At the beginning of the story, the family was not recycling. At the end of the story, they were recycling.

Let's Compare! You Really Should Recycle (page 116)

Students' letters will vary but should support their ideas about recycling with information specific to the texts.

Nonfiction Text Teacher Notes
Recycling Trends

	Lesson Steps	Teacher Think Alouds
Ready, Set, Predict!	• Provide the text to students and display a larger version. Allow them time to predict what it will be about. • Ask partners to identify and respond to the text feature that is included in the text using the following: *I think the graph will _____.*	"When I see graphs included with a text, I think about how they can help me better understand the text."
Go!	• Allow time for students to read through the text independently. • Read the text aloud to students. Model how to read the graph aloud. • Discuss how to read the graph both to understand it and also how to read it aloud. Write the following sentence frame on the board: *In _____ (year), _____ percent of aluminum cans were recycled.*	"When a graph is included in a text that I am reading aloud, I have to put the information in the graph into sentence form such as *In 1985, a little more than 50 percent of aluminum cans were recycled.*"
Reread to Clarify	• Have students reread the text independently and circle words or ideas they want to clarify. • Ask students to box the words that tell about what types of materials can be recycled.	
Reread to Question	• Assign each pair of students a year from the graph. Ask partners to reread the text and write questions about the percentage of recycled aluminum cans or the year using the following: *In what year was _____ percent of cans recycled? What percent of cans were recycled in _____?* • Have students respond to the question and prompts on page 112.	
Reread to Summarize and Respond	• Tell students to reread the text to summarize. Have them write short summaries that tell about the graph in the text. Ask them to add sentences to their summaries that tell about their predictions for aluminum recycling for the next five years.	"When I see a graph with trends such as this one, I try to predict what may happen in the future."

*Note: For more tips, engagement strategies, and fluency options to include in this lesson, see pages 122–128.

Recycling Trends

Many things can be recycled. This includes, but is not limited to, aluminum cans, plastic bottles, glass, paper, newspaper, and tin cans. Look at this chart showing the percentages of aluminum cans collected for recycling since 1975.

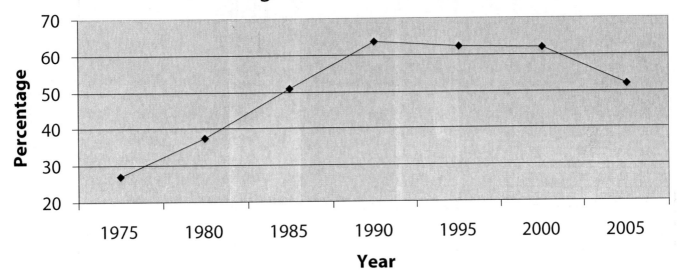

Percentage of Aluminum Cans Recycled

"Recycling Trends" Response

Directions: Reread the text on page 111 to answer each question.

1. What year was the peak year for recycling aluminum cans?

    Ⓐ 2000   Ⓒ 1980

    Ⓑ 1990   Ⓓ 2005

2. A trend is defined as a general direction. Describe the trend shown on the graph.

_____

_____

_____

_____

_____

3. The graph only shows the percentages of aluminum cans recycled. What other items does the text say can be recycled?

_____

_____

_____

_____

_____

Fiction Text Teacher Notes
Over and Over Again

	Lesson Steps	Teacher Think Alouds
Ready, Set, Predict!	• Provide the text to students and display a larger version. Have students skim the text and predict what the text will be about. • Ask partners to respond to the following: *I think I know _____ about recycling.*	"When I see the text is about recycling, I think about all the things I already know about recycling."
Go!	• Allow time for students to read the text. Encourage them to box words they don't know. • Read the text aloud to students as you model fluency. Discuss how you change your voice in the reading and how that helps with comprehending the passage. • Invite students to reread the text with partners as they practice trying to use different voices for the characters.	
Reread to Clarify	• Have students reread the text and circle any words or phrases they want to clarify. Give time for partners to discuss strategies for clarifying the words and phrases. • Ask students to underline words that allow them to visualize what Ann and her family do to set up recycling at their house. Have students draw pictures to support what they read.	
Reread to Question	• Divide students into small groups. Distribute an index card to each group. Have them reread the text and write questions on their cards using the following: *In what ways do _____?* Collect the questions. Ask the questions aloud to the class and tell groups to work together to answer them. • Have students respond to the question and prompts on page 115.	"In what ways do Mom and Dad support Ann's excitement for recycling?"
Reread to Summarize and Respond	• Reread the title to students. Ask students to reread the text to summarize. Have them evaluate whether or not they think the title is a good one. Have students work in small groups to think of other appropriate titles. Gather the suggestions together, and invite the class to vote on the best title.	"The title of a text usually tells what the text will be about. This title describes what this text is about because recycling is about using things over and over again."

***Note:** For more tips, engagement strategies, and fluency options to include in this lesson, see pages 122–128.

Over and Over Again

At school, Ann learned about recycling. She learned that metal, paper, plastic, and glass can be reused!

Ann told Mom and Dad about recycling. They agreed to recycle. They found bins. They had a bin for paper. They had one for metal. And they had one for plastic and glass. They put the bins in the garage.

Dad said, "We will use these every day." Ann and her family cared about helping Earth.

Each day, they used the bins. Newspapers, boxes, and milk jugs went in. Bottles, cans, and jars were put in them. Then the bins were full. Ann and her mom took them to a recycling center. The old things would become new again!

"Over and Over Again" Response

Directions: Reread the text on page 114 to answer each question.

1. Which item is **not** named in the text as being able to be recycled?

   Ⓐ plastic   Ⓒ paper

   Ⓑ glass   Ⓓ wood

2. Why did the family get motivated to recycle?

   _____

   _____

   _____

   _____

   _____

3. How have Ann and her family changed by the end of the story?

   _____

   _____

   _____

   _____

Social Studies Texts

Let's Compare!

You Really Should Recycle

Directions: Write a letter to your family or someone else who does not recycle to convince them they should. Include information about setting up their house for recycling, why they should recycle, and trends in recycling. Use information from both "Over and Over Again" and "Recycling Trends" to help you.

Dear _____

_____

_____

_____

_____

_____

_____

_____

_____

_____

_____

_____

_____

                                            _____

Name: _____   **Date:** _____

Thinking About Recycling!

Directions: Choose at least two of these activities to complete.

Radical Reading

Practice reading "Over and Over Again" using different voices for each character. Perform your version for a friend.

Fun Fluency

Work with a partner to rewrite "Over and Over Again" as a reader's theater script or as a jingle. Add dialogue for the different characters. Practice and perform what you write.

Wonderful Words

Write the word *recycle* at the top of a sheet of paper. Create as many words as you can using the letters in *recycle*. Assign yourself two points for two-letter words, three points for three-letter words, etc. Total up your points. Try to get at least 20 points.

Wacky Writing

Write a slogan to help you tell others how important it is to recycle. Create a poster and include the slogan on it. Add pictures, too! Share your poster with your family.

References Cited

Brassel, Danny, and Timothy Rasinski. 2008. *Comprehension that Works: Taking Students Beyond Ordinary Understanding to Deep Comprehension*. Huntington Beach, CA: Shell Education.

Common Core State Standards Initiative. 2010. *Common Core State Standards for English Language Arts & Literacy in History/Social Studies, Science, and Technical Subjects*. Washington, DC: National Governors Association Center for Best Practices and the Council of Chief State School Officers.

Fisher, David, and Nancy Frey. 2012. "Close Reading in Elementary Schools." *The Reading Teacher* 66 (3): 179–188.

Hattie, John A. 2008. *Visible Learning*: *A Synthesis of Over 800 Meta-Analyses Relating to Achievement*. Oxford, UK: Routledge.

Oczkus, Lori D. 2010. *Reciprocal Teaching at Work: Powerful Strategies and Lessons for Improving Reading Comprehension 2nd Edition*. Newark, DE: International Reading Association.

Oczkus, Lori D. 2012. *Just the Facts: Close Reading and Comprehension of Informational Text*. Huntington Beach, CA: Shell Education and International Reading Association (copublication).

Palincsar, Annemarie Sullivan, and Ann L. Brown. 1986. "Interactive Teaching to Promote Independent Learning from Text." *The Reading Teacher* 39 (8): 771–777.

Rasinski, Timothy V. 2010. *The Fluent Reader: Oral and Silent Reading Strategies for Building Fluency, Word Recognition and Comprehension 2nd Edition*. New York: Scholastic.

Rasinski, Timothy V. and Lorraine Griffith. 2010. *Building Fluency Through Practice and Performance*. Huntington Beach, CA: Shell Education.

Rosenshine, Barak, and Carla Meister. 1994. "Reciprocal Teaching: A Review of the Research." *Review of Educational Research* 64 (4): 479–530.

Correlation to the Standards

Shell Education is committed to producing educational materials that are research and standards based. In this effort, we have correlated all of our products to the academic standards of all 50 states, the District of Columbia, the Department of Defense Dependents Schools, and all Canadian provinces.

How to Find Standards Correlations

To print a customized correlation report of this product for your state, visit our website at http://www.shelleducation.com and follow the on-screen directions. If you require assistance in printing correlation reports, please contact our Customer Service Department at 1-877-777-3450.

Purpose and Intent of Standards

Legislation mandates that all states adopt academic standards that identify the skills students will learn in kindergarten through grade twelve. Many states also have standards for Pre–K. This same legislation sets requirements to ensure the standards are detailed and comprehensive.

Standards are designed to focus instruction and guide adoption of curricula. Standards are statements that describe the criteria necessary for students to meet specific academic goals. They define the knowledge, skills, and content students should acquire at each level. Standards are also used to develop standardized tests to evaluate students' academic progress. Teachers are required to demonstrate how their lessons meet state standards. State standards are used in the development of all of our products, so educators can be assured they meet the academic requirements of each state.

Common Core State Standards

The activities in this book are aligned to the Common Core State Standards (CCSS). The chart on page 120 lists the standards addressed in each lesson. Specific standards are also listed on the first page of each lesson.

McREL Compendium

We use the Mid-Continent Research for Education and Learning (McREL) Compendium to create standards correlations. Each year, McREL analyzes state standards and revises the compendium. By following this procedure, McREL is able to produce a general compilation of national standards. Each lesson in this product is based on one or more McREL standards. The chart on page 121 lists the standards addressed in each lesson.

TESOL and WIDA Standards

The activities in this book promote English language development for English language learners. The chart on page 121 lists the standards addressed in each lesson.

Next Generation Science Standards

This set of national science standards aims to incorporate knowledge and process standards into a cohesive framework. The chart on page 121 lists the standards addressed in each lesson.

Correlation to the Standards (cont.)

College and Career Readiness Standards	Lessons
Literacy.RL.3.1—Ask and answer questions to demonstrate understanding of a text, referring explicitly to the text as the basis for the answers.	School Lunches (p. 28); Multiplication (p. 37); Mountain Heights (p. 46); Veterans Day (p. 91)
Literacy.RL.3.2—Recount stories, including fables, folktales, and myths from diverse cultures; determine the central message, lesson, or moral and explain how it is conveyed through key details in the text.	Life Cycles (p. 73)
Literacy.RL.3.3—Describe characters in a story (e.g., their traits, motivations, or feelings) and explain how their actions contribute to the sequence of events.	Helen Keller (p. 19); Measurement (p. 55); Storms (p. 64); Gravity (p. 82); Recycling (p. 109)
Literacy.RL.3.5—Refer to parts of stories, dramas, and poems when writing or speaking about a text, using terms such as chapter, scene, and stanza; describe how each successive part builds on earlier sections.	Benjamin Franklin (p. 10); Susan B. Anthony (p. 100)
Literacy.RI.3.1—Ask and answer questions to demonstrate understanding of a text, referring explicitly to the text as the basis for the answers.	Helen Keller (p. 19); Multiplication (p. 37); Susan B. Anthony (p. 100)
Literacy.RI.3.2—Determine the main idea of a text; recount the key details and explain how they support the main idea.	School Lunches (p. 28)
Literacy.RI.3.3—Describe the relationship between a series of historical events, scientific ideas or concepts, or steps in technical procedures in a text, using language that pertains to time, sequence, and cause/effect.	Storms (p. 64); Veterans Day (p. 91)
Literacy.RI.3.4—Determine the meaning of general academic and domain-specific words and phrases in a text relevant to a grade 3 topic or subject area.	Gravity (p. 82)
Literacy.RI.3.5—Use text features and search tools (e.g., key words, sidebars, hyperlinks) to locate information relevant to a given topic efficiently.	Benjamin Franklin (p. 10); Mountain Heights (p. 46)
Literacy.RI.3.7—Use information gained from illustrations (e.g., maps, photographs) and the words in a text to demonstrate understanding of the text (e.g., where, when, why, and how key events occur).	Measurement (p. 55); Recycling (p. 109)
Literacy.RI.3.8—Describe the logical connection between particular sentences and paragraphs in a text (e.g, comparison, cause/effect, first/second/third in a sequence).	Life Cycles (p. 73)
Literacy.RF.3.4.a—Read on-level text with purpose and understanding.	Benjamin Franklin (p. 10)
Literacy.RF.3.4.b—Read on-level prose and poetry orally with accuracy, appropriate rate, and expression on successive readings.	School Lunches (p.28)
Literacy.RF.3.4.c—Use context to confirm or self-correct word recognition and understanding, rereading as necessary.	Helen Keller (p. 19)

Correlation to the Standards (cont.)

McREL Standards	Lessons
Science 5.1—Knows that plants and animals progress through life cycles of birth, growth and development, reproduction, and death; the details of these life cycles are different for different organisms.	Life Cycles (p. 73)
Science 10.2—Knows that the Earth's gravity pulls any object toward it without touching it.	Gravity (p. 82)
Geography 16.5—Knows advantages and disadvantages of recycling and reusing different types of materials.	Recycling (p. 109)
History 4.3—Understands how people over the last 200 years have continued to struggle to bring all groups in American society the liberties and equality promised in the basic principles of American democracy.	Susan B. Anthony (p. 100)
History 4.8—Understands the events and democratic values commemorated by major national holidays.	Veterans Day (p. 91)
Math 2.4—Understands the basic meaning of place value.	Mountain Heights (p. 46)
Math 3.1—Multiplies and divides whole numbers.	Multiplication (p. 37)
Math 4.1—Understands the basic measures perimeter, area, volume, capacity, mass, angle, and circumference.	Measurement (p. 55)

Next Generation Science Standards	Lessons
3-ESS3-1.B—A variety of natural hazards result from natural processes. Humans cannot eliminate natural hazards but can take steps to reduce their impact.	Storms (p. 64)

TESOL/WIDA Standards	Lessons
English language learners **communicate** for **social, intercultural,** and **instructional** purposes within the school setting	All Lessons
English language learners **communicate** information, ideas, and concepts necessary for academic success in the area of **language arts**	All Lessons
English language learners **communicate** information, ideas, and concepts necessary for academic success in the area of **mathematics**	All Mathematics Lessons
English language learners **communicate** information, ideas, and concepts necessary for academic success in the area of **science**	All Science Lessons
English language learners **communicate** information, ideas, and concepts necessary for academic success in the area of **social studies**	All Social Studies Lessons

Tips for Implementing the Lessons

Lesson Tips

Below are additional tips and suggestions you may wish to use with students as you implement the lessons.

- Choose 4 to 6 words from each text pair and place them on a word wall for students to observe. Students can complete various word activities with the words.

- Use online resources, such as video clips or audio clips, to help students better understand the content.

- Have students research the authors of some of the texts or research more about the content in the texts so students can gain more knowledge.

- Keep a running list of strategies students use to clarify words, phrases, and ideas. Have the list visible for students to use as they clarify texts (e.g., reread, read on, sound out).

- Choose a long word from a text and present the letters of the word to students in alphabetical order, dividing the letters into consonants and vowels. Guide students to make a series of 5 to 10 words with the letters by giving them word meanings or clues to guess the words.

- Play WORDO with students by having them draw 4 x 4 matrixes. Display 16 to 20 words from the texts. Have students write one word in each box. Randomly select a word and call out its definition. Have each student mark the box the word is in. The first student to get four words in a straight or diagonal line calls out, "Wordo!"

- Invite students to act out words, sentences, or main ideas of a text with or without using their voices. Have the rest of the class guess what is being acted out.

Pacing Tips

Below are suggested options for implementing the lessons with students.

An Ideal Pacing Plan	If Working with Longer Texts
Day 1: Nonfiction text close reading lesson/follow-up activities	**Day 1:** Complete the close reading steps, including predicting, clarifying, questioning, and summarizing, for the first portion of the text.
Day 2: Fiction text close reading lesson/ follow-up activities	
Day 3: Compare the texts/follow-up activities	**Day 2:** Running through all four steps again for the second portion of the text.
Day 4: Reread texts/follow-up activities	**Note:** The follow-up activities should be done at the conclusion of the entire reading of a text.
Day 5: Reread texts/share follow-up activities	

Strategies

Engagement Strategies

Make learning memorable by using the following engagement strategies.

Discussion in Pairs

Throughout the lessons, have students talk with partners or groups to enhance comprehension. Conduct whole-group sharing after partners discuss their responses.

Mark or Code with Text Symbols

Have students work independently or in groups to mark the text using symbols to show their thinking. Provide copies of the text for students and display a copy of the text for the class to view as you demonstrate. Symbols may include:

  + main idea   √ details   # cool idea   ☺ favorite part

Have students use different colored pencils, highlighters, or markers as they read. They can circle, underline, or box portions of the text.

Discussion Sentence Frames

Have students use discussion sentence frames when sharing responses with others. Frames help keep students on task during discussions. Some examples include:

Predict	**Clarify**
I think I will learn _____ because_____. *I think the author wrote this because _____.*	*I didn't get the word/sentence _____, so I _____.*
Question	**Summarize**
Who, what, when, where, why, how, I wonder _____.	*This is about _____.* *The main idea is _____.*

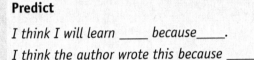

Close Reading Props

Bring in a pair of goofy glasses or a magnifying glass to hold up when it is time to read a text closely. You may wish to duplicate the glasses or magnifying glass patterns found on page 126 for students to use during the lessons.

Glasses	**Magnifying Glass**
Tell students, "Close reading is like putting on special glasses as you reread the text to figure it out."	Tell students, "Close reading is like using a magnifying glass to help you understand the text as you reread it."

Sing to the Strategies

Help students remember the different purposes for rereading by creating a song with verses for each of the reciprocal teaching strategies. A song option can be found on page 128.

Strategies (cont.)

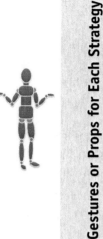

Gestures or Props for Each Strategy

Use gestures or props to help students remember the close reading strategies as they closely read a text.

Predict: Use a physical crystal ball or pretend to rub a crystal ball to predict what will happen or what the text is about using clues from the text.	**Question:** Use a physical microphone or use a fist to make a microphone to interview one another asking and answering questions.
Clarify: Use glasses or a magnifying glass. You can also use your arms: parallel to show a "pause" button, point to the left for rewind, and to the right for reading on to help clarify tricky words in a text.	**Summarize:** Use a lasso (with yarn or string) or pretend to wield a lasso to rope in the "main ideas and details" of a text.

Adapted from Lori Oczkus (2010)

Fluency Strategies

The chart below lists various fluency techniques to use with students.

Model Fluent Reading	Teacher or other proficient reader reads the text to students. After the reading, teacher leads students in a discussion of the content of the text *and* the way in which the teacher or reader reads the text (e.g., expression, phrasing, pacing).
Assisted Reading— Choral Reading	Groups of students read the text orally together. Students who are more fluent readers provide an assist to students who are less fluent.
Assisted Reading— Paired Reading	Two readers read a text orally together. One reader is more proficient than the other. The more proficient reader acts as a model for the less fluent one.
Assisted Reading— Audio-recorded Reading	A student reads a text while at the same time listening to a fluent recording of the same text. The recorded reading acts as a model for the student.
Assisted Reading— Echo Reading	Teacher reads the text aloud while tracking the print for students to see. After the text has been read aloud, children imitate, or echo, the teacher as they visually track the text.
Repeated Reading	Students read a text several times orally and silently for different purposes. One purpose for all rereading is to improve students' fluency (e.g., word recognition, automaticity, and expression).
Phrased Text Reading	The teacher or student marks the appropriate phrase boundaries in a text with slash marks. The student then reads the text, pausing at the marked locations. Readers who lack fluency often read in a word-by-word manner that limits the meaning of the passage. These visual cues give students support in reading in meaningful phrases.

Adapted from Timothy Rasinski (2010)

Assessment Options

Aside from students' work on the activity pages, there are many opportunities to assess students during each step of the close reading process. Use the chart below to guide your assessments.

Ready, Set, Predict!

Does the student . . .
- skim the text/visuals to make logical predictions?
- relate relevant prior knowledge?
- anticipate author's purpose?
- predict topic/theme?
- anticipate how the text is organized?

Go!

Does the student . . .
- make an attempt to read the text independently?
- follow along during the teacher read-aloud?
- mark unfamiliar words and ideas?
- participate in shared readings; follow along?
- identify what makes the teacher's reading fluent?

Reread to Clarify

Does the student . . .
- reread to mark words they want to know or clarify?
- identify words/lines that help students visualize?
- identify more than one "fix it" strategy such as sounding out, chopping words into parts, rereading, reading on?

Reread to Question

Does the student . . .
- reread to ask or create questions for peers?
- reread to answer text-dependent questions using text evidence?
- confidently ask and answer questions?

Reread to Summarize and Respond

Does the student . . .
- select main ideas and details to summarize?
- summarize selection in order?
- use key vocabulary to summarize?
- mark text to show responses using symbols?

  + main idea   √ details   # cool idea   ☺ favorite part

- compare/contrast the fiction and nonfiction texts?

Templates

Glasses

Directions: Decorate the glasses. Then, cut them out and glue them on a craft stick. Use them as you closely read text.

Magnifying Glass

Directions: Decorate the magnifying glass. Then, cut it out and use it as you closely read text.

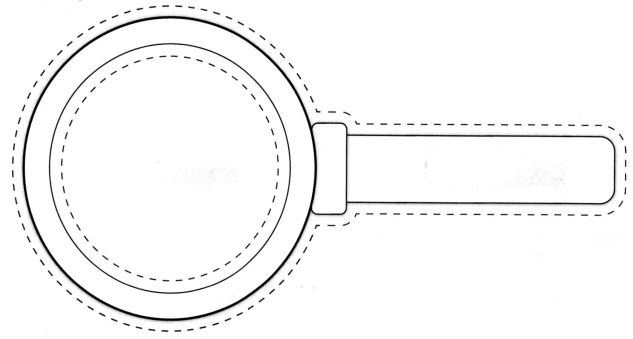

Close Reading Bookmarks

Ready, Set, Predict!
- Skim over the text and visuals.
- Predict what the text is about.
- Talk to a partner.

Go!
- Read the text once by yourself.
- Then listen to the teacher read.
- Mark words you want to know.

Reread to Clarify
- Read the text again.
- Mark more tricky words/ideas.
- Talk to a partner about your words.

Reread to Question

- Read the text again.
- Stop and ask questions.
- Share questions with a partner.
- Use text evidence to ask and answer questions.

Reread to Summarize and Respond

- Read the text again.
- Mark parts of the text to show what you are thinking.

+ main idea	√ details
# cool idea	☺ favorite part

- Share the main idea/details with a partner.

Ready, Set, Predict!
- Skim over the text and visuals.
- Predict what the text is about.
- Talk to a partner.

Go!
- Read the text once by yourself.
- Then listen to the teacher read.
- Mark words you want to know.

Reread to Clarify
- Read the text again.
- Mark more tricky words/ideas.
- Talk to a partner about your words.

Reread to Question

- Read the text again.
- Stop and ask questions.
- Share questions with a partner.
- Use text evidence to ask and answer questions.

Reread to Summarize and Respond

- Read the text again.
- Mark parts of the text to show what you are thinking.

+ main idea	√ details
# cool idea	☺ favorite part

- Share the main idea/details with a partner.

Read it Again: Sure to Win!

Lyrics by Timothy Rasinski

(Sung to the tune of "Take Me Out To The Ball Game")

Here's a tip for your reading—
Here's a tip: prediction!
Skim through the passage now, more or less,
Then you can form a pretty good guess!
Then, it's read, read, read through the passage;
Did your prediction come true?
Read it once, twice, maybe three times
To make sense to you!

Here's a tip for your reading—
Here's a tip: read again!
Hard words and tricky parts you may spy,
Read it once more to help clarify!
So, just read, read, read through your passage.
You're sure to win if you do!
Read it once, twice, maybe three times
To make sense to you!

Here's a tip for your reading—
Here's a tip: read again!
Read it, and then you a question ask;
Look to the text to help in this task!
So, just read, read, read through your passage,
You're sure to win if you do!
Read it once, twice, maybe three times
To make sense to you!

Here's a tip for your reading—
Here's a tip: read again!
Then read it once more to summarize
All the main parts are before your eyes.
So, just read, read, read through your passage,
You're sure to win if you do!
Read it once, twice, maybe three times
To make sense to you!

#51359—*Close Reading with Paired Texts* © *Shell Education*